New Directions in Irish and Irish
American Literature

Series Editor
Claire A. Culleton
Department of English
Kent State University
Kent, OH, USA

New Directions in Irish and Irish American Literature promotes fresh scholarship that explores models of Irish and Irish American identity and examines issues that address and shape the contours of Irishness and works that investigate the fluid, shifting, and sometimes multivalent discipline of Irish Studies. Politics, the academy, gender, and Irish and Irish American culture, among other things, have not only inspired but affected recent scholarship centered on Irish and Irish American literature. The series's focus on Irish and Irish American literature and culture contributes to our twenty-first century understanding of Ireland, America, Irish Americans, and the creative, intellectual, and theoretical spaces between.

More information about this series at
http://www.palgrave.com/gp/series/14747

Vincent J. Cheng

Amnesia and the Nation

History, Forgetting, and James Joyce

Vincent J. Cheng
University of Utah
Salt Lake City, UT, USA

New Directions in Irish and Irish American Literature
ISBN 978-3-030-10117-6   ISBN 978-3-319-71818-7   (eBook)
https://doi.org/10.1007/978-3-319-71818-7

Cover credit: LPETTET and traffic_analyzer

Printed on acid-free paper

This Palgrave Macmillan imprint is published by Springer Nature
The registered company is Springer International Publishing AG
The registered company address is: Gewerbestrasse 11, 6330 Cham, Switzerland

*For my family—Maeera, Gabi,
Mom, TC, and Chiqui—
and the memory of my father*

PREFACE

This book is a study of the relationships between memory, history, and the nation—relationships that have preoccupied me, as well as our contemporary culture, for some time. Most particularly, it explores the roles forgetting and amnesia play in forming national identities and histories—in a series of particular case studies and through interdisciplinary analysis of a number of modernist literary texts, especially the works of the great Irish writer James Joyce, but also a number of other literary texts by Milan Kundera, Ford Madox Ford, F. Scott Fitzgerald, and Walker Percy. Drawing on thinkers such as Friedrich Nietzsche, Karl Marx, Ernest Renan, Sigmund Freud, A.R. Luria, Benedict Anderson, and Yosef Yerushalmi, this study explores the burden of the past, a past that one would like to forget and extinguish. More generally, the book's two central focuses are Ireland and the American South, both burdened with the "nightmare of history"—from the Battle of the Boyne to the Good Friday Agreement, from the Civil War to the 2015 Mother Emanuel killings in Charleston, South Carolina.

Chapter 1 ("Introduction: Memory, Forgetting, and the Imagination") begins by noting that amnesia—as a neurological condition—is always represented as a negative thing, a loss of a personal identity that one desperately needs to recover. Much scholarly and scientific work has been done, in recent decades, on issues having to do with memory, Alzheimer's, trauma, remembrance, memorials and monuments, truth and reconciliation. But hardly anyone ever talks about the desirability or usefulness of forgetting—which is a central concern of this study. Drawing on Nietzsche, Marx, Renan, Freud, Luria, Anderson, Yerushalmi, and others, this introductory chapter considers the importance of forgetting—and then goes on to consider the complex relationships between remembering, forgetting, imagination, desire, and narrative.

William Faulkner wrote famously that in the American South "The past is never dead. It's not even past." The second chapter ("The Nightmare of History and the Burden of the Past") discusses how, for the modern world, the past seems a burden that one—whether an individual or a community—has to carry around in the present. Many modern thinkers have been thus engaged in a "memory crisis" arising out of this obsession with the power—and the burden—of the past, what Milan Kundera calls "the burden of memory." This chapter goes on to explore the issues involved in trying to extinguish the past (and the memory of the past)—focusing particularly on Joyce's and Kundera's novels, but also on novels by Ford Madox Ford, F. Scott Fitzgerald, and Walker Percy—within Nietzsche's and Renan's arguments about the desirability of forgetting.

Chapter 3 ("The Will to Forget: Nation and Forgetting in *Ulysses*") begins with a discussion of Ernest Renan's influential 1882 lecture "What Is a Nation?" and its argument for the importance of national forgetting to the peace and unity of a nation-state, and then focuses on one particular literary case study, Joyce's treatments of these issues in *Ulysses*. The second half of this chapter continues pursuing the complex realities of national "memory" and the nation-state—by considering the role of "place" and "space" in Irish memory and the Irish national imaginary through a series of controversies about the nature of "Irishness" and the Irish nation, from the eighteenth century to the 1998 Good Friday Agreement in Northern Ireland.

The fourth chapter ("The Memory of the Past: National Memory and Commemoration") takes up two case studies involving Irish national memory and commemoration. The first explores the ways that Joyce's works—from "The Dead" to *Finnegans Wake*—treat the historical memory of William III, Prince of Orange (and his horse) at the Battles of Aughrim and the Boyne, the events that sealed the future of Ireland as a British colony and as an island of divided allegiances (orange vs. green), with Unionists revering the memory of King Billy and Republicans despising it. The second case study takes up a more recent battle, the 1916 Easter Rising, and explores the varying and conflicting ways that it has been remembered for the past 100 years, including during the recent 2016 centenary commemorations.

The last two chapters focus on the American South, most particularly the relationship between the Irish and Southern American history. Chapter 5 ("Joyce, Ireland, and the American South: Whiteness, Blackness, and Lost Causes") explores the historical connections between Ireland and the American South—particularly the shared dedication to lost causes, the role of Irish nationalism and Irish immigration in the formation of Irish American identity, and the divisiveness of racial issues involving the Civil War and slavery. The Irish—considered racially "other" at the time, *not* white—nevertheless managed to become accepted by Southern natives as white Southerners, so much so that *Gone with the Wind*, the most influential cultural representation of Southern culture of the Civil War era, could have its heroine (Scarlett O'Hara) be the daughter of an Irish immigrant whose Southern white status is not even questioned. The chapter discusses how this union between Irishness and Southernness came about—and explores Joyce's depictions of the South in several of his works, concluding with a discussion of the opening pages of *Finnegans Wake*, which have much to say about the Irish presence in the South, the Ku Klux Klan, and racial strife.

Chapter 6 ("Slavery, the South, and Ethical Remembrancing") probes the ethics of historical memory by considering two contemporary developments having to do with Southern race hatred, slavery, and the complex dynamics of remembering and commemorating problematic histories in our contemporary moment: the killings by Dylann Roof at the Emanuel African Methodist Episcopal Church in Charleston, South Carolina; and the recent revelations about Georgetown University's slaveholding past (having to do with Irish Jesuit priests) and the University's current attempts to come to terms with that past.

Throughout this book, I explore the complexities, nuances, and ethical issues involved in the processes of historical memory and national identity. A brief Afterword reconsiders the relationships between history and narrative, between the historical past and interpretive/imaginative fiction, and what is at stake in these matters at our contemporary moment.

Salt Lake City, UT, USA   Vincent J. Cheng

Acknowledgments

Several people have been instrumental in helping me develop this project at different stages. I would like to thank Oona Frawley and Katherine O'Callaghan, and also Michèle Mendelssohn, for publishing essays of mine that first helped me formulate and articulate this project. Later, it was Joe Kelly's invitation to give the keynote address at the 2013 James Joyce Conference in Charleston, South Carolina, that inspired me to start thinking about the Irish in the South—and which eventually led to both Chaps. 5 and 6. Joe Kelly, Margot Norris, and Viet Nguyen have been generous and astute readers of this manuscript, and I am very grateful to them—as I am also to Claire Culleton for her support and encouragement as series editor of the Irish and Irish American Literature series at Palgrave Macmillan. I am grateful to my colleagues at the University of Utah for their sharp observations and helpful comments on different chapters-in-progress; and for the University of Utah Faculty Fellowship which allowed me, during 2011–2012, the release time to begin working on this project in earnest. Finally, I am most grateful to Maeera Shreiber—my best reader, interlocutor, and supporter.

* * *

Some of the material in both Chaps. 1 and 3 was adapted from two earlier essays of mine which helped launch this book project—and which appeared in *James Joyce and Cultural Memory*, eds. Oona Frawley and Katherine O'Callaghan (Syracuse: Syracuse University Press, 2014), and in *21st-Century Approaches to Literature: Late Victorian into Modern, 1880–1920,* eds. Laura Marcus, Michele Mendelssohn and Kirsten Shepherd-Barr (Oxford: Oxford University Press, 2016). A short passage from Chap. 2 was adapted from two pages in my earlier book, *Shakespeare and Joyce: A Study of "Finnegans Wake"* (University Park: Penn State University Press, 1984); and another section of Chap. 2 was adapted from an essay of mine in *Praharfeast: James Joyce in Prague*, eds. David Vichnar, David Spurr and Michael Groden (Prague: Litteraria Pragensia Books, 2012). A couple of passages in Chap. 3, and a small passage in Chap. 5, were adapted from material in my book *Inauthentic: The Anxiety Over Culture and Identity* (New Brunswick: Rutgers University Press, 2004). And finally, a couple of passages in Chap. 4 were adapted from my earlier book *Joyce, Race, and Empire* (Cambridge: Cambridge University Press, 1995) and from an essay of mine in *A Portrait of the Artist as a Young Man: Case Studies in Contemporary Criticism*, ed. R.B. Kershner (Bedford/St. Martin's Press, 2005). I am grateful for having been granted permission to reuse material from these earlier publications of mine.

CONTENTS

Abbreviations

Quotations from the following works by James Joyce are cited in the text through these abbreviations:

CW *The Critical Writings of James Joyce*. Ed. Ellsworth Mason and Richard Ellmann. New York, Viking 1959.

D *Dubliners: Text, Criticism, and Notes*, eds. Robert Scholes and A. Walton Litz. New York: Viking, 1969.

FW *Finnegans Wake*. New York: Viking, 1939.

P *A Portrait of the Artist as a Young Man: Text, Criticism, and Notes*, ed. Chester G. Anderson. New York: Viking, 1968.

SH *Stephen Hero*. Eds. John J. Slocum and Herbert Cahoon. New York: New Directions, 1959.

U *Ulysses*. Eds. Hans Walter Gabler et al. New York: Vintage, 1986.

Passages from *Ulysses* are identified by episode and line number. Quotations from *Finnegans Wake* are identified by page and line number. Citations from the other texts above are identified by page number. These conventions generally follow the format prescribed by the *James Joyce Quarterly*.

LIST OF FIGURES

CHAPTER 1

Introduction: Memory, Forgetting, and the Imagination

AMNESIA AND THE WILL TO FORGET

Let me begin on a personal note. Although I am known among my family and friends for having a good memory, I have long been aware, since my childhood, of the attractions, even the desirability, of forgetting. Indeed, in my teens and twenties, I used to regularly experience what I grew to call "amnesia fantasies"—that is, wish-fulfillment fantasies in which I imagined that I found myself suffering from amnesia, and having no idea who I was. In that condition, I could be, of course, unburdened of my own troubles, and free to move on. I suspect I am not alone in having had such fantasies: after all, who has not, in periods of unhappiness, wished to be someone else—or at least wished to be able to slough off one's own past and identity and what Joyce's Stephen Dedalus refers to as the nightmare of history? And what more attractive and dramatic fantasy—even more attractive perhaps than Freud's "family romance"—than to obliterate one's own personal past and identity by finding oneself an amnesiac?

Of course, the discourses of Western culture are always enjoining us to *remember*, not to forget, warning us instead about the dangers of forgetting: those who don't remember the past are doomed to repeat it; the Holocaust enjoins Jews to "never forget," just as the Hebrew Bible reminded them always to remember Zion, even by the rivers of Babylon; we are each urged to remember our roots, our identity; trauma victims are

© The Author(s) 2018
V. J. Cheng, *Amnesia and the Nation*, New Directions in Irish and Irish American Literature, https://doi.org/10.1007/978-3-319-71818-7_1

1

coaxed into recovering repressed memories so that they may heal and move on; and so on. Hardly anyone ever talks about the desirability or usefulness of forgetting. Indeed, amnesia—as a neurological condition—is always represented as a negative thing, a loss of a personal identity that one desperately needs to recover. After all, one's identity is basically constituted of one's memories: the ultimate version of an amnesia fantasy is, arguably, Alzheimer's disease, which in its advanced stages constitutes both the total loss of memory and the total loss of identity.

But I would suggest that our culture also has a collective fascination with amnesia. Actual amnesia, as a medical condition, is an extremely rare occurrence. Yet, in popular culture it is an extremely *frequent* occurrence, almost ubiquitous. Stories of amnesiacs are the stuff of spy novels, mystery novels, popular films, television soap operas, science fiction, sensational tabloid journalism, and so on. Think, for example, of the popularity in recent years of the novels and films of *The Bourne Supremacy, The Bourne Identity, The Bourne Ultimatum,* and *Jason Bourne*; other recent films like *Memento* and *The Eternal Sunshine of the Spotless Mind*; a host of mystery, science fiction, and psychological novels with titles like *Amnesia, Amnesia Moon,* and so on; the wide international news coverage given a few years ago to that Englishman who disappeared in a canoe in the North Sea, then turned up five years later claiming to have lost his memory; in fact, the very first episode, in 1973, of the daytime television staple *The Young and the Restless* was a story about an amnesiac. One could go on and on with examples of our collective cultural fascination with amnesia—in spite of the fact that almost no one has ever personally met or known an actual amnesiac.[1] What is it about amnesia that is so fascinating—and even attractive—to our collective consciousness? Is it a trope for something deeper, something repressed? At the very least, what this phenomenon suggests to me is that we have, in fact, a cultural *will to forget*— a compulsive attraction/fascination for the idea of a clean slate. This notion, and the corollary ability to remake oneself, certainly is a long-standing and defining tradition at least in American history, from Benjamin Franklin to the novels of Horatio Alger to F. Scott Fitzgerald's *The Great Gatsby*. It is as if we have a need (even if in fantasy) to erase one's past from one's memory.

One of the most famous and defining examples of clinical amnesia was the case of the World War II soldier who was shot in the head at the Battle of Smolensk. The great Russian psychologist Alexandr Romanovitch Luria told his story in a book titled *The Man with a Shattered World: The History of a Brain Wound*; Luria also recorded a very different case history in a second book called *The Mind of a Mnemonist: A Little Book about a Vast Memory*. The two cases are almost mirror-images of each other as opposites: the story of the wounded, amnesiac soldier, and the story of a man who remembered virtually everything, the mnemonist. The first we understand as a tragic pathology. But, as the great Jewish philosopher and historian Yosef Yerushalmi writes: "Yet the phenomenon of the mnemonist was no less pathological. If the brain-damaged man could not remember, the mnemonist could not forget. And so it was even difficult for him to read, not because, like the man of Smolensk, he had forgotten the meaning of words, but because each time he tried to read, other words and images surged up from the past and strangled the words and text he held in his hands" (Yerushalmi 106). This is sensory and mnemonic overload (what today we might call "information overload"): the world and the text are both too crammed with remembered meanings for the individual to function. As Luria himself notes: "Many of us are anxious to find ways to improve our memories; none of us have to deal with the problem of how to forget. In [this man's] case, however, precisely the reverse was true. The big question for him, and the most troublesome, was how he could learn to forget" (*Mind* 67).

The mnemonist's haunting dilemma, I would suggest, is not unlike that confronted by James Joyce's character Stephen Dedalus, and indeed by the Irish people, in the face of a traumatic colonial history: "History," says Stephen in *Ulysses*, "is a nightmare from which I am trying to awake" (*U* 2.377). To describe history as a nightmare from which one wants to awake implies a complex relationship between the past, trauma, suffering, sleep, waking, forgetting, memory, amnesia, and repression. Similarly, as I have argued elsewhere, "for Stephen and his fellow Irishmen imperial history is very much an oppressive nightmare of the present from which it is hard to awake—if for no other reason than that its oppressive presence and hegemonic, discursive terminology is written all over the face of Ireland and of its cultural constructions, and thus forms the [unavoidable] hour-by-hour subtext and context of all their thought and experiences" (*Joyce, Race, and Empire*, 169)—as, for example, in the "Hades" episode of *Ulysses*, as the funeral carriage conveys the Irishmen first past the statue of William Smith O'Brien, a patriotic hero of the failed rebellion of 1848, then past "the hugecloaked Liberator's form" (*U* 6.249), Daniel O'Connell's statue; then "Nelson's pillar" (*U* 6.293), the hated English imperial symbol; then the "Foundation stone for Parnell" (*U* 6.320; now the Parnell Memorial in Parnell Square); and so on. The streets of Dublin—like the streets of many cities and towns in the American South, similarly filled with statues and memorials to the Confederate dead and their failed leaders—become themselves a concrete text which one is never allowed to forget, a constant reminder of one's oppressive colonial past and one's continued colonial subservience, denying the attractions of forgetting, denying the possibility of any relief from the nightmare of history. As with the mnemonist, the inability to forget and the sensory overload of too much memory produce an agonizing paralysis, a nightmare from which one cannot awaken.

In his essay "On the Uses and Disadvantages of History for Life" (first published in 1874), Friedrich Nietzsche remarked that "life in any true sense is absolutely impossible without forgetfulness":

> [W]e must know the right time to forget as well as the right time to remember, and instinctively see when it is necessary to feel historically and when unhistorically. This is the point that the reader is asked to consider: that the unhistorical and the historical are equally necessary to the health of an individual, a community, and a system of culture. (Cited in Yerushalmi 107)

But, if health lies somewhere between total remembering and amnesia, between the mnemonist and the soldier in Smolensk, what is the right balance? As Yerushalmi asks: "[G]iven the need both to remember and to forget, where are the lines to be drawn? ... How much history do we require? What kind of history? What should we remember, what can we afford to forget, what must we forget? These questions are as unresolved today as they were then; they have only become more pressing" (107).

What should we forget, and what should we remember? And *when* should we forget, and when remember? If both activities are important to the health of an individual, they are perhaps also both important to the health of a nation or a people. Which of the two is the more important, which is the greater danger? Yerushalmi himself is unequivocal on this issue. Asked to consider what might be the "Uses of Forgetting," he writes: "In the Hebrew Bible they are not to be found. The Bible only knows the terror of forgetting. Forgetting, the obverse of memory, is always negative, the cardinal sin from which all others will flow." (108) The key Biblical text, Yerushalmi suggests (108), is to be found in the eighth chapter of Deuteronomy:

Beware lest you *forget* the Lord your God so that you do not keep His commandments and judgments and ordinances ... lest you lift up your hearts and *forget* the Lord your God who brought you out of the land of Egypt, out of the house of bondage ... And it shall come to pass if you indeed *forget* the Lord your God ... I bear witness against you this day that you shall utterly perish. (Deut. 8:11, 14, 19)[2]

On the other hand, Ernest Renan—as we shall see—has argued memorably that a nation's unity depends on the process of forgetting—and that for purposes of a nation's collective well-being, some things are better forgotten: "Unity is always effected by means of brutality .... Yet the essence of a nation is that all individuals have many things in common; and also that they have forgotten many things .... It is good for everyone to know how to forget" (11, 16).

REMEMBERING AND THE IMAGINATION

Memory studies has become an increasingly important and crowded field in recent decades—and much scholarly and scientific work has been done on issues having to do with memory, Alzheimer's, trauma, remembrance, memorials and monuments, truth and reconciliation. Some of the most important recent studies include: Maurice Halbwachs, *The Collective Memory* (1980); Pierre Nora, *Les Lieux de Memoire* (1997); Yosef Hayim Yerushalmi, *Zakhor: Jewish History and Jewish Memory* (1996); James E. Young, *The Texture of Memory: Holocaust Memorials and Meaning* (1993); Lawrence L. Langer, *Admitting the Holocaust: Collected Essays* (1995); Cathy Caruth (ed.), *Trauma: Explorations in Memory* (1995); Benedict Anderson, *Imagined Communities: Reflections on the Origin and Spread of Nationalism* (1983); Edward S. Casey, *Remembering: A Phenomenological Study* (1987); Paul Ricoeur, *Memory, History, Forgetting* (2004); Paul Connerton, *How Modernity Forgets* (2009); Anne Whitehead, *Memory* (2009); *Theories of Memory: A Reader* (2007), edited by Michael Rossington and Anne Whitehead; and many others. Much of the current interest and scholarship within memory studies has been further fueled in recent years by the sub-fields of trauma studies and Holocaust studies. And now there is increasing interest in the study of forgetting: not only are doctors and scientists developing the "emerging science of forgetting" (www.newsweek.com/health-life-science-forgetting-77209), but theorists and scholars of memory have become increasingly interested not just in remembering but also in the phenomenon of forgetting (see especially Casey, Whitehead, and Connerton).

Remembering and forgetting are, of course, intimately related: indeed, one requires the existence of the other. Edward S. Casey refers to "forgetting as the primary other of memory" (Casey xi), reminding us that "in order to remember together, we must first forget together" (xii); when we mourn someone at his or her funeral, we are not only honoring and invoking the memory of the deceased, but at the same time "the mourners are sanctioning each other *to begin to forget the deceased*—to 'lay her to rest'" (xii). In the same way, Casey notes, Freud had pointed out (in "Mourning and Melancholia") that after a dear one's death "we bring up memories of that person and hypercathect them—only to decathect them shortly after: the intensification of active remembrance is precisely what allows for the de-intensification of forgetfulness" (xii). Indeed, one might even argue that attempts to preserve the memory of something are equally attempts to achieve the relief of forgetting. Pierre Nora points out that in "delegating to the *lieu de memoire* [the place of memory, such as monuments and statues] the responsibility of remembering, [memory] sheds its signs upon depositing them there, as a snake shed its skin" (cited in Young 181). As James E. Young notes: "In shouldering the memory-work, monuments may relieve viewers of their memory burden …. To the extent that we encourage monuments to do our memory-work for us, we become that much more forgetful. In effect, the initial impulse to memorialize events like the Holocaust may actually spring from an opposite and equal desire to forget them" (Young 181).

Indeed, remembering and forgetting were once thought to be literally related: the Greek goddess Mnemosyne was the goddess of memory, while her sister Lesmosyne was the goddess of forgetting. Nowadays Lesmosyne (whose name is etymologically related to Lethe, the river of forgetfulness) has been herself forgotten. Both sisters once occupied a high station in Western thought and cosmology. Mnemosyne was the mother of the muses—and thus the origin of all human culture and cultural activities, including art, literature, history, and the sciences. For memory was considered the wellspring of all these endeavors.

That is because the Greeks had what Casey calls an "activist" view of memory as an active and transformative process of imaginative recreation—"according to which memory involves the creative transformation of experience rather than its internalized reduplication in images or traces construed as copies" (Casey 15). Casey argues that, unfortunately, our contemporary world has bought into a "passivist" paradigm of memory, seeing all mnemonic activities as merely involving a process of retrieval and replication—for we tend to regard the past "as something merely 'fixed' and 'dead'"—and thus "we have turned in recent times to machines as repositories and models of memory" (4):

> Where once Mnemosyne was a venerated Goddess, we have turned over responsibility for remembering to the cult of the computers, which serve as our modern mnemonic idols. The force of the remembered word in oral traditions—as exemplified in feats of bardic recounting that survive only in the most isolated circumstances—has given way to the inarticulate hum of the disk drive. Human memory has become self-externalized: projected outside the rememberer himself or herself and into non-human machines. These machines, however, *cannot remember*; what they can do is to record, store, and retrieve information—which is only part of what human beings do when they enter into a memorious state. (Casey 2)

The activist tradition, on the other hand, views memory-work not as a straightforward process of retrieval, but rather—in John Rickard's words—as "a creative or active search back through language and experience guided by the imagination and as dependent on the context of the present as on the past"; as with Freud's later writings, Rickard notes, the activist tradition "sees memory as an intersection between actual experience and interpretation, imagination, and repression" (Rickard 10). Which is to say that memory, in the activist paradigm, negotiates between experience, imagination, and forgetfulness; memory is at once therapy and imaginative reconstruction and reinterpretation. Put another way, memory is "reading."

What is our relationship with our past experiences? Does memory freeze them in the unchanging past (as the passivist tradition would have it)? Or is the past not actually retrievable but is, rather, malleable, changeable, and subject to interpretation or reconstruction? Every time we remember something, are we to some extent rewriting the past? Is memory-work a passive act of information retrieval, or is it an active, transformative process of imaginative reconstruction? Casey argues for this latter view:

> The situation is such that remembering transforms one kind of experience into another: *in being remembered, an experience becomes a different kind of experience*. It becomes "a memory," with all that this entails, not merely of the consistent, the enduring, the reliable, but also of the fragile, the errant,

the confabulated. Each memory is unique; none is simple repetition or revival. The way that the past is relived in memory assures that it will be transfigured in subtle and significant ways …. Remembering is itself essential to what is happening, part of every action, here as well as elsewhere: "remembrance is always now." (xxii)

In other words, remembering is always a creative, transformative, and ongoing process; which is to say that remembering is a narrative act.

This accords well with the conclusions Freud reached late in his career (Casey points out that psychoanalysis is engaged "in a continuous struggle against the forces of forgetfulness" [8]). Indeed Freud, over time, moved increasingly from a confidence in the centrality of the primal scene as retrievable and necessary for a cure, and gradually focused increasingly on the activities of narrative in order to explain the past. As Whitehead points out, in *The Psychopathology of Everyday Life* (1901) Freud sketches out a view of memory not as a set of original impressions but as the process of remembering itself: "The past is no longer inert and passive, but is powerfully reshaped in and through the concerns of the present. The delayed action of remembering, in other words, allows the past to develop, to evolve along with changing circumstances over time. In the face of this more complex and shifting memory process, the task of the analyst is no longer one of straightforward recovery but of reconstruction, which provides a narrative of the past not as it was but as it might have been" (Whitehead 91). Freud's notion of a "talking cure" entails a tight relationship between remembering, dialogue, and narration. And this process of individual self-narration was, in the later Freud, analogous to the collective process of narrating the nation. As Ned Lukacher points out in *Primal Scenes: Literature, Philosophy, Psychoanalysis*: "Freud writes that the narrative construction through which an individual creates its identity involves 'a complicated process of remodeling analogous in every way to the process by which a nation constructs legends about its early history'" (19). By 1937, Freud (in "Constructions in Analysis") goes so far as to write that the analyst's mission is "to make out what has been forgotten from the traces which it has left behind or, more correctly, to *construct* it" (Rickard 50).

In other words, for Freud memory became increasingly a form of *reading* the past—rather than a straightforward retrieval of the past. For the later Freud, the past was both readable and writable. As with a national mythology, constructing a viable narrative of one's personal past allows the patient to go on and live a healthy life—which is to say that a coherent narrative of the past is necessary for a healthy future (this conclusion, as we shall, has its real-life analogue in the situation and dilemma of actual amnesiacs). This is the model of memory which John Frow posits as based on "textuality" (Frow, *Time* 228)—in which memory is no longer just a recovery of traces of the past, but rather a reconstruction of the past under the circumstances of the present. In this model, meaning is provided retroactively in a process of ongoing interpretation. As Anne Whitehead puts it, "Memory, in this instance, is no longer related to the past as a form of truth but as a form of desire" (Whitehead 49). Both memory and psychoanalysis entail a creative act of imagination, both involve a "reading" of one's life in an interpretive process of narration. Both, in short, are versions of writing fiction.

FORGETTING AND THE IMAGINATION

If remembering involves the ongoing exercise of imagination and narrative, where does forgetting fit in? Casey reminds us that the oral recitations of long poems by ancient Greek poets (in prodigious feats of memory) was "a way of getting (and staying) in touch with a past that would otherwise be consigned to oblivion: it was a fateful fending off of forgetfulness" (12). So it would seem that forgetting would be the antithesis of the creative (and poetic) use of memory. But Casey notes further that "the past to which the bard transported his audience was more mythical than historical" and that "to be conveyed into this past is to be able to forget, however briefly, the anxieties of the present"; in this way "forgetting and remembering work hand-in-hand, each helping the other to realize an optimal form" (12). In other words, the creation and performance of literature here is an act of willful forgetting (of the anxieties of the present)—an observation that, we might note, parallels something we are all, as readers, very familiar with: the attraction of literature (and reading) as a mode of escape from the reader's own present, a form of mental voyaging and imaginative escapism, a willed forgetting of the reality of the present, of the here and now.[3] Forgetting thus becomes integral to the creative exercise of memory—as reconstruction, as narrative. "Indeed," Casey reminds us, "for the early Greeks generally, forgetting and remembering form an indissociable pair; they are given explicit mythical representation in the coeval figures of Lesmosyne and Mnemosyne, who are conceived as equals *requiring* each other" (12). Thus a study of memory, of remembering, is also necessarily a study of forgetting. As Whitehead points out, forgetting "not only forms the shadowy underside of memory but, more precisely, shapes and defines the very contours of what is recalled and preserved; what is transmitted as remembrance from one generation to the next; and what is thereby handed down to us, in our turn, to cherish or discard, but above all to reflect critically upon" (Whitehead 14).

A desire to forget the *present* (at least temporarily) is at the root of the activity of reading (as a form of desire) and the consequent attraction of literature as a form of mental voyaging. Similarly, a desire to forget the *past* is at the root of the will to forget that I have dubbed "amnesia fantasies," an urge to forget that allows for the creation of alternative possibilities to fill the vacuum.[4] In either case, forgetting is itself central to the narrative reconstruction of the past and of one's memories; forgetting spawns, and makes room for, imagination and the new. In short, the activity of forgetting (whether conscious or unconscious) is at the source of both narrative and remembering, and thus at the source of literature itself.

Such a conception of both remembering and forgetting as an ongoing narration and reconstruction of the past is very much the vision/logic of memory that John Frow advocates as "the logic of textuality" and which he contrasts to the passivist model of memory he labels "the logic of the archive": "The time of textuality is not the linear, before-and-after, cause-and-effect time embedded in the logic of the archive but the time of a continuous analeptic and proleptic shaping" (Frow, *Toute* 154). In such a model, Frow suggests, the past is never already written: "rather than having a meaning and a truth determined once and for all by its status as event, its meaning and its truth are constituted retroactively and repeatedly; if time is reversible then alternative stories are always possible." This is the logic of history and narrative as the creation of infinite possibilities (as I will argue in Chap. 2). Such a model is able to account for forgetting as a key function: "Forgetting is thus an integral principle of this model, since the activity of compulsive interpretation that organizes it involves at once selection and rejection. Like a well-censored dream, and subject perhaps to similar mechanisms, memory has the orderliness and the teleological drive of narrative. Its relation to the past is not that of truth but of desire" (154). Memory and forgetting, in short, are both intimately connected to imagination, narrative, and desire.

NOTES

1. As Joyce Carol Oates writes, "[A]mnesia has become a crowded literary terrain. Rare in life, amnesia abounds in contemporary literature and in the most stylish contemporary movies." Oates goes on to note that "[t]he attraction of waking not to the usual flood of memories and associations like dirty dishwater but to a tabula rasa of infinite possibility is obvious, especially in a debased political/cultural era" (Oates 1). Jonathan Lethem similarly points out: "Amnesiacs might not much exist, but amnesiac characters stumble everywhere through comic books, movies, and our dreams"; amnesia, he points out, is "a floating metaphor very much in the air" (Lethem xiii).

2. These are Biblical lines and injunctions which, of course, were also significant to the Irish nationalist movement in Joyce's day, imagining itself as Israelites remembering Zion so that they might emerge out of the house of bondage. See Abby Bender, *Israelites in Erin: Exodus, Revolution, and the Irish Revival.*

3. As Keats writes in the "Ode to a Nightingale": "Fade far away, dissolve, and quite forget / What thou among the leaves hast never known, /The weariness, the fever, and the fret / Here, where men sit and hear each other groan ..."

4. As Oates points out, such a fantasy "holds irresistible attractions for both writer and reader since it seems to replicate the mysterious and seductive adventure of the yet-unwritten/yet-unread text" (1).

WORKS CITED

Anderson, Benedict. *Imagined Communities: Reflections on the Origin and Spread of Nationalism.* Revised edition. London: Verso, 1991.

Bender, Abby. *Israelites in Erin: Exodus, Revolution, and the Irish Revival.* Syracuse, NY: Syracuse University Press, 2015.

Bhabha, Homi K., ed. *Nation and Narration.* London: Routledge, 1990.

Casey, Edward S. *Remembering: A Phenomenological Study.* Second Edition. Bloomington: Indiana University Press, 2000.

Cheng, Vincent J. *Joyce, Race, and Empire.* Cambridge: Cambridge University Press, 1995.

Connerton, Paul. *How Modernity Forgets.* Cambridge: Cambridge University Press, 2009.

Frow, John. *Time and Commodity Culture: Essays in Cultural Theory and Postmodernity.* Oxford: Clarendon Press, 1997.

———. From "'*Toute la memoire du monde:* Repetition and Forgetting.'" In Rossington and Whitehead 150–156.

Joyce, James. *Ulysses.* Eds. Hans Walter Gabler et al. New York: Vintage, 1986.

Lethem, Jonathan. *The Vintage Book of Amnesia.* New York: Random House, 2000.

Lukacher, Ned. *Primal Scenes: Literature, Philosophy, Psychoanalysis.* Ithaca, NY: Cornell University Press, 1986.

Luria, A. R. *The Mind of a Mnemonist: A Little Book about a Vast Memory.* New York: Basic Books, 1968.

———. *The Man with a Shattered World: The History of a Brain Wound.* Cambridge, MA: Harvard University Press, 1972.

Nietzsche, Friedrich. *From* "On the Uses and Disadvantages of History for Life." In Rossington and Whitehead 102–108.

Nora, Pierre. *Les lieux de mémoire,* vol. I. Paris: Editions Gallimard, 1997.

Oates, Joyce Carol. "Lest We Forget." *The New York Review of Books* (July 19, 2007): www.nybooks.com/articles/2007/07/19/lest-we-forget/

Renan, Ernest. "What Is a Nation?" Trans. Martin Thom. In Homi K. Bhabha, ed., *Nation and Narration.* 8–22.

Ricoeur, Paul. *Memory, History, Forgetting.* Trans. Kathleen Blamey and David Pellauer. Chicago: University of Chicago Press, 2004.

Rickard, John S. *Joyce's Book of Memory: The Mnemotechnic of Ulysses.* Durham, NC: Duke University Press, 1999.

Rossington, Michael and Anne Whitehead, editors. *Theories of Memory: A Reader.* Baltimore: Johns Hopkins University Press, 2007.

Whitehead, Anne. *Memory.* New York: Routledge, 2009.

Yerushalmi, Yosef Hayim. *Zakhor: Jewish History and Jewish Memory.* New York: Schocken Books, 1989.

Young, James E. From *The Texture of Memory: Holocaust Memorials and Meaning.* In Rossington and Whitehead 177–184.

CHAPTER 2

The Nightmare of History and the Burden of the Past

Happiness? That's nothing more than good health and a poor memory.
—*Albert Schweitzer*

IN DEFENSE OF FORGETTING

William Faulkner wrote famously that in the American South, "[t]he past is never dead. It's not even past" (*Requiem for a Nun*, 92). Indeed, for the modern world, the past is a burden that one—whether an individual or a community—has to carry around. Many twentieth-century thinkers have been thus engaged in a "memory crisis" arising out of this obsession with the power—and the burden—of the past. Freud of course (and psychoanalysis generally) was fascinated with the power of the past over the present, but as Anne Whitehead points out, Freud became increasingly aware that "[a]nalysis cannot remove the burden of the past, which we are fated to always carry within us ... for we cannot simply 'extinguish' the memory of the past; all of our attempts to do so are, indeed, paradoxically greeted by its more aggressive revival or return" (101).

Friedrich Nietzsche and also, as we will see later, Ernest Renan, two late nineteenth-century thinkers, have been among the few advocates of forgetting, of the need to forget in the face of the burdens of history and memory. Karl Marx too, in his essay "The Eighteenth Brumaire of Louis Bonaparte" (1852), discusses how the burden of the past haunts and dictates the present, specifically how the French "could not free themselves

© The Author(s) 2018
V. J. Cheng, *Amnesia and the Nation*, New Directions in Irish and Irish American Literature, https://doi.org/10.1007/978-3-319-71818-7_2

of the memory of Napoleon" (99). Marx thus advocates a turning against memory: "The social revolution of the nineteenth century can only create its poetry from the future, not from the past" (99). For, as Marx writes famously in the opening of his essay, "[t]he tradition of the dead generations weighs like a nightmare on the minds of the living" (97)—a line often translated more directly as "[h]istory weighs like a nightmare upon the brain of the living."

James Joyce's character Stephen Dedalus echoes Marx's statement when, in the "Nestor" episode of *Ulysses*, he complains that "[h]istory ... is a nightmare from which I am trying to awake" (*U* 2.377). Joyce's writings are threaded through obsessively by the nightmare and burden of history on turn-of-the-century Irish culture, at both the individual and the national levels. Indeed, Stephen might well have been prone to what I referred to earlier as "amnesia fantasies"—that is, wish-fulfillment fantasies in which one could feel unburdened by one's own troubles, and thus free to move on—fantasies of being able to slough off one's own past and identity and the nightmare of history. Stephen's desire is for a form of what Milan Kundera, in *The Unbearable Lightness of Being*, calls "lightness," specifically a form of amnesia that erases the nightmare of the past and the burdens of history, allowing for new and other imaginative possibilities.

Stephen's personal dilemma is also the collective dilemma of the Irish people in the face of a traumatic colonial history. As I argued earlier, for Stephen and his fellow Irishmen imperial history is very much still a nightmare of the present moment, from which it is hard to awake—for its oppressive, discursive presence is visible all over the face of Ireland and of its cultural constructions, and thus "forms the [unavoidable] hour-by-hour subtext and context of all their thought and experiences" (Cheng, *Joyce* 169). In this way, the streets of Dublin become themselves a concrete text one is not allowed to forget, reminding one of their oppressive colonial past and their continuing colonial subservience. The attractions of forgetting and any relief from the nightmare of history are thus beyond reach; and so the inability to forget and the sensory overload of too much memory produce an agonizing paralysis, a nightmare from which one cannot awaken.

In contrast to the streets of Joyce's Dublin, the streets of Prague—as described by Milan Kundera in *The Book of Laughter and Forgetting* (1979)—are sites of forgetting, of the loss of memory and history: "Prague in [Kafka's] novels," Kundera writes, "is a city without memory. It has even forgotten its name .... Time in Kafka's novels is the time of humanity that has lost all continuity with humanity, of a humanity that no longer knows anything nor remembers anything, that lives in nameless cities with nameless streets or streets with names different from the ones they had yesterday, because a name means continuity with the past, and people without a past are people without a name." In Kundera's own novel, written during the Communist era, Prague is similarly a city suffering from a collective, national amnesia: "There are all kinds of ghosts prowling these confused streets. They are the ghosts of monuments demolished – demolished by the Czech Reformation, demolished by the Austrian Counterreformation, demolished by the Czechoslovak Republic, demolished by the Communists. Even statues of Stalin have been torn down. All over the country, wherever statues were thus destroyed, Lenin statues have sprouted up by the thousands. They grow like weeds on the ruins, like melancholy flowers of forgetting" (*Book*, 157–58). While Joyce's Dublin is full of monuments recording its long history of colonialism and the burdens of memory and the past, Kundera's Prague is a palimpsest of forgotten histories and vanished monuments.

*   *   *

Stephen's thoughts in the "Nestor" episode of *Ulysses* are revealing in terms of this tension between history/memory and potential future possibilities. In the opening lines of the episode, Stephen, teaching a history lesson to his class of young schoolboys, thinks of history as a destroyer, an ouster of possibilities. This notion is introduced when Stephen comments on the "pier" which a student in his class referred to in his confusion over the name of Pyrrhus: "Kingstown pier, Stephen said. Yes, a disappointed bridge" (2.39). "How sir?" a student asks. A disappointed bridge, perhaps, simply because it *is* a pier—therefore severely limited in scope, the possibility of its being a bridge having been ousted by its clearly being a pier. Actual, factual history makes it so. Stephen Dedalus is himself remorseful because of the memory of his dead mother and the hurt he gave her. Her death is fact, and history makes it so; thus, his guilty memories and "agenbite of inwite" (remorse of conscience) cannot be absolved—for she is dead, and nothing can change that absolute fact of history and the painful burden of his memory. This is why, to the aspiring young artist struggling over "love's bitter mystery" (1.240), history is such a nightmare—because of its destructive qualities:

Had Pyrrhus not fallen by a beldam's hand in Argos or Julius Caesar not been knifed to death. They are not to be thought away. Time has branded them and fettered they are lodged in the room of the infinite possibilities they have ousted. But can those have been possible seeing that they never were? Or was that only possible which came to pass? (2.48–52)

In these crucial lines, Stephen is referring to Aristotle's notion in the *Metaphysics* ("Aristotle's phrase" in 2.68) that there is a room of infinite possibilities, of untapped potential—if Caesar had not been knifed to death, he might have lived to a ripe old age, might have developed cancer, might even have come to America—but history limits, and chooses from that room one possibility (which is that Caesar gets knifed to death), thus destroying all others. History, then, is seen by Stephen as a usurper and a destroyer of creative potential, a restrictive force which limits other, perhaps more interesting possibilities. Stephen goes on to quote Milton:

–*Weep no more, woful shepherds, weep no more*
For Lycidas, your sorrow, is not dead,
Sunk though he be beneath the watery floor ...
    It must be a movement then, an actuality of the possible as possible.
(2.64–66)

To Stephen (as also to Aristotle; see *Poetics* 8:4–9:2), the conflict lies between history and poetry: Lycidas's death is a historical fact; other possibilities are ousted by that certainty. The poet Milton, however, asserts that Lycidas is *not* dead; whereas factual history eliminates possibilities, poetry forges and creates new and other possibilities. Thus the poet and the imagination are placed in the role of revivifiers, re-creators, constructive counters to history's destructiveness: "It must be a movement then, an actuality of the possible as possible." A passive acceptance of history and memory can be countered by an active exercise of imagination and potential. The question is one of control: does history control us by limiting our possibilities and rendering us slaves to the burdens of memory? Or do we control history and memory by creating new and different possibilities, by interpreting both history and memory in light of the needs of the present? Does the father create the son; or the son, the father?[1]
    Nietzsche similarly regarded history as a burden we inevitably carry around and which weighs us down. In his essay "On the Uses and Disadvantages of History for Life" (first published in 1874), Nietzsche expresses an envy of cattle for their ignorance of history and memory, for their consequent happiness which is based on their continual forgetting:

"Consider the cattle, grazing as they pass you by: they do not know what is meant by yesterday or today, they leap about, eat, rest, digest, leap about again, and so from morn till night and from day to day, fettered to the moment and its pleasure or displeasure, and thus neither melancholy nor bored" (101). A human being, by contrast, is weighed down by the crushing and accumulated weight of the past. As a result, Nietzsche suggests, a human envies the cattle's obliviousness to history and memory: "for though he thinks himself better than the animals because he is human, he cannot help envying them their happiness—what they have, a life neither bored nor painful, is precisely what he wants." For "the man says 'I remember' and envies the animal, who at once forgets and for whom every moment really dies, sinks back into night and fog and is extinguished for ever. Thus the animal lives *unhistorically*: for it is contained in the present."

For Nietzsche, as for Marx, happiness is to live in the present moment, unburdened by the nightmare which weighs on the brain of the living, and is defined by the "ability to forget": "In the case of the smallest or of the greatest happiness, however, it is always the same thing that makes happiness happiness: the ability to forget or, expressed in more scholarly fashion, the capacity to feel *unhistorically* during its duration" (103). Thus, memory is the enemy of inner peace, for the burden of a remembered history causes paralysis: "He who cannot sink down on the threshold of the moment and forget all the past … Will never know what happiness is … he would in the end hardly dare to raise his finger" (103). Thus, forgetting is necessary to happiness: "Forgetting is essential to action of any kind, just as not only light but darkness too is essential for the life of everything organic" (103). Memory and "the historical sense" are detrimental equally to a person or to a society, for "it is altogether impossible to *live* at all without forgetting … *whether this living thing be a man or a people or a culture*" (104; emphasis in the original).

As a result, Nietzsche advocates a practice of "active forgetfulness," a willed forgetting. Responding to the crushing burden of history, Nietzsche thus writes a defense of forgetting, in particular the forgetting of history. In the end, Nietzsche suggests, both remembering and willed/active forgetting—what Nietzsche calls the "historical" and the "unhistorical"—are necessary to the health and happiness of an individual, as well as of a nation:

> Cheerfulness, the good conscience, the joyful deed, confidence in the future—all of them depend, in the case of the individual as of a nation, … on one's being just as able to forget at the right time as to remember at the right time; on the possession of a powerful instinct for sensing when it is

necessary to feel historically and when unhistorically. This, precisely, is the proposition the reader is invited to meditate upon: *the unhistorical and the historical are necessarily in equal measure for the health of an individual, of a people and of a culture.* (104; emphases in the original)

*   *   *

In his novel *The Unbearable Lightness of Being*, Milan Kundera refers to Nietzsche's ideas in introducing the dualities—heaviness and lightness—which dominate and obsess his book. Like Nietzsche, Kundera too is concerned with the burden of the past and of remembrance. In citing Nietzsche's concept of "eternal return," Kundera seems to agree with Nietzsche that recollecting the past is an intolerable burden:

In the world of eternal return the weight of unbearable responsibility lies heavy on every move we make. That is why Nietzsche called the idea of eternal return the heaviest of burdens (*das schwerste Gewicht*).
    If eternal return is the heaviest of burdens, then our lives can stand out against it in all their splendid lightness. (*Unbearable* 5)

Kundera's contrasting notions of heaviness and lightness thus seem connected to Nietzsche's views on memory and forgetting, on the burden and weight of memory and history that necessitates the relief of forgetting. Heaviness for Kundera is related to both the intolerable burdens of "love's bitter mystery" and to the "nightmare" of history (specifically, in the novel, the stifling oppression in Czechoslovakia under Communist rule), those heavy realities—both personal and national—from which one would wish to escape from into amnesia or oblivion. "Splendid lightness," on the other hand, is made possible by forgetting and by freedom from those weighty burdens. Kundera asks: "But is heaviness truly deplorable and lightness splendid?"

For Nietzsche, forgetfulness is the necessary and desired relief from the intolerable burdens of "love's bitter mystery" and the nightmare of history; for Kundera, on the other hand, lightness, the ability to be free of one's heavy burdens, renders one only partially real (just as amnesiacs are deprived of their identity and "realness"):

The heaviest of burdens crushes us, we sink beneath it, it pins us to the ground. But in the love poetry of every age, the woman longs to be weighed down by the man's body. The heaviest of burdens is therefore simultaneously

an image of life's most intense fulfillment. The heavier the burden, the closer
our lives come to the earth, the more real and truthful they become.

Conversely, the absolute absence of a burden causes man to be lighter
than air, to soar into the heights, take leave of the earth and his earthly being,
and become only half real, his movements as free as they are insignificant. (5)

Kundera goes on to ask: "Which then shall we choose? Weight or lightness?" In Edward S. Casey's view, the choice Kundera proposes can be
interpreted thus: "[W]hat will we choose—the way of remembering or the
way of forgetting? ... Might we then take seriously once more the genuine
weight of memory instead of mindlessly opting for the spurious lightness
of forgetting?" (Casey 4).

In Kundera's novel, this choice—"weight or lightness?"—takes the
form of the question repeatedly confronting the main character Tomas
about his love and his feelings of responsibility for his lover Tereza: "Was
it better to be with Tereza or to remain alone?" (8) As Kundera points out,
"When we want to give expression to a dramatic situation in our lives, we
tend to use metaphors of heaviness. We say that something has become a
great burden to us. We either bear the burden or fail and go down with it,
we struggle with it, win or lose" (122). Tomas's own instincts and desires
run toward lightness, preferring to engage in short-term love affairs unen-
cumbered by any personal commitment, responsibility, or emotional connection: "thus in practically no time he managed to rid himself of wife,
son, mother, and father" (12); "the unwritten contract of erotic friendship
stipulated that Tomas should exclude all love from his life" (13). Sabina,
his mistress, and Tereza, the woman who loves him and wants him exclu-
sively for her own, embody this choice between lightness and heaviness:
"Tereza and Sabina represented the two poles of his life, separate and
irreconcilable, yet equally appealing" (28). Sabina herself seeks to live a life
with no strings attached, no burdens or responsibilities: "Her drama was a
drama not of heaviness but of lightness. What fell to her lot was not the
burden but the unbearable lightness of being" (122); "Tereza and Tomas
had died under the sign of weight. [Sabina] wanted to die under the sign
of lightness. She would be lighter than air" (273).

Kundera, however, sides with heaviness, suggesting that it is the more
"real" condition: "The heavier the burden, the closer our lives come to the
earth, the more real and truthful they become." The "splendid lightness"
that comes from forgetting, while it can relieve the burdens of existence,
in fact leaves us feeling only "half real" and "lighter than air," "insignificant" and unsubstantial. The heaviness of memory and responsibility, on

the other hand, connects us to others and grounds us in truthfulness and emotional depth. Kundera depicts, in the course of the novel, how Tomas's and Tereza's love grows in substance and weight because they learn to accept the burden and responsibility for each other over time—in spite of Tomas's ongoing desire for lightness. Thus, while Kundera agrees with Nietzsche and Stephen Dedalus that the burdens of memory and responsibility are crushingly heavy and that consequently the lightness of forgetting is desirable, for Kundera memory and heaviness also carry an ethical dimension and a moral responsibility: for a life of lightness in our modern world would be more "unbearable" than to carry, like Atlas, the heavy burden of one's responsibilities.

*   *   *

Stephen Dedalus's case, and the cases of Tomas and Tereza in Kundera's novel, are instances of individuals struggling with *personal* issues of memory and forgetting. But both Joyce and Kundera are also concerned with the parallel issues on the collective and national levels. National forgetting, however, is a convenient luxury of the winners. It is clearly beneficial to the unity of a sovereign state or empire—in Kundera's case, the Soviet empire—for its subjects to be able to forget the history of bloody conquest and empire-building if they are to partake in a collective identity as members of such sovereignty. But such collective, national amnesia—at both the individual and the national levels—is precisely what Kundera takes issue with in his earlier (1979) novel, *The Book of Laughter and Forgetting*. Kundera opens the novel by describing a famous photograph taken on the 21st of February1948, in which Czech Communist leader (and later President) Klement Gottwald "stepped out on the balcony of a Baroque palace in Prague to address the hundreds of thousands of his fellow citizens packed into Old Town Square. It was a crucial moment in Czech history" (*Book* 3). Standing next to Gottwald was his fellow politician Vladimir Clementis: "There were snow flurries, it was cold, and Gottwald was bareheaded. The solicitous Clementis took off his own fur cap and set it on Gottwald's head" (3). The famous photograph taken of that moment showed Gottwald speaking on the balcony, fur cap on head and Clementis by his side; thousands of copies of the photograph were then distributed by the Communist Party's propaganda machine: "On that balcony the history of Communist Czechoslovakia was born. Every child knew the photograph from posters, schoolbooks, and museums" (3). But when, four years later, Clementis was charged with treason and hanged, the Party's propaganda section immediately airbrushed him out of all the photographs—and out of history: "Ever since, Gottwald has stood on that balcony alone. Where Clementis once stood, there is only bare palace wall. All that remains of Clementis is the cap on Gottwald's head" (3).

In the novel, Kundera's characters—including Mirek—suffer under "the burden of memory" (187); like Stephen Dedalus, Mirek wishes to forget or erase the personal past. Twenty-five years earlier Mirek had had an affair with an ugly woman named Zdena and now wished to erase all memories of her ("he was particularly gratified to note that he had completely forgotten their copulations" [5]): "The reason he wanted to remove her picture from the album of his life was not that he hadn't loved her, but that he had. By erasing her from his mind, he erased his love for her. He airbrushed her out of the picture in the same way the Party propaganda section airbrushed Clementis from the balcony where Gottwald gave his historic speech" (21). Here, Kundera's narrator correlates individual with national amnesia in a shared urge to erase the burdens of the past, the individual urge implicating the national (and vice versa): "Mirek is as much a rewriter of history as the Communist Party, all political parties, all nations, all men. People are always shouting they want to create a better future. It's not true. The future is an apathetic void of no interest to anyone. The past is full of life, eager to irritate us, provoke and insult us, tempt us to destroy or repaint it. The only reason people want to be masters of the future is to change the past" (22).

Mirek himself is aware of the parallels, for "it is 1971, and Mirek says that the struggle of man against power is the struggle of memory against forgetting" (7). The repainting/forgetting of the past is being practiced by the Communist Party to try to erase the memory of dissension and forge an imagined national unity:

> And just to be sure not even the shadow of an unpleasant memory could come to disturb the newly revived idyll, both the Prague Spring and the Russian tanks, that stain on the nation's history, had to be nullified. As a result, no one in Czechoslovakia commemorates the 21st of August, and the names of the people who rose up against their own youth are carefully erased from the nation's memory, like a mistake from a homework assignment. (14)[2]

Similarly, Kundera points out that "Husak, the seventh president of my country, is known as *the president of forgetting*" for dismissing some 145 Czech historians from universities and research institutes who were deemed to be threats to the regime's control over both ideology and memory. As one of these historians, a character in Kundera's novel, points out: "The first step in liquidating a people … is to erase its memory. Destroy its books, its culture, its history. Then have somebody write new books, manufacture a new culture, invent a new history. Before long the nation will begin to forget what it is and what it was. The world around it will forget even faster" (159).

After all, "in times when history moved slowly, events were few and far between and easily committed to memory" (7); but the modern world—with its speed, technology and information overload—makes it very easy to forget things: "The bloody massacre in Bangladesh quickly covered over the memory of the Russian invasion of Czechoslovakia, the assassination of Allende drowned out the groans of Bangladesh, the war in the Sinai Desert made people forget Allende, the Cambodian massacre made people forget Sinai, and so on and so forth until ultimately everyone lets everything be forgotten" (7). Our contemporary world is one where historical amnesia is motivated by the nightmare of history—and is assisted by a memory (and information) overload.

In a 1980 interview with Philip Roth, Kundera, notes that—in the wake of a half-century during which Czechoslovakia experienced "democracy, fascism, revolution, Stalinist terror, as well as the disintegration of Stalinism, German and Russian occupation, mass deportations, [and] the death of the West in its own land"—the nation "is thus sinking under the weight of history" (*Book* 231). But this nightmare of history must not allow one to forget that forgetting itself "is also the great problem of politics":

> When a big power wants to deprive a small country of its national consciousness it uses the method of *organized forgetting*. This is what is currently happening in Bohemia. Contemporary Czech literature, insofar as it has any value at all, has not been printed for twelve years; 200 Czech writers have been proscribed, including the dead Franz Kafka; 145 Czech historians have been dismissed from their posts, history has been rewritten, monuments demolished. A nation which loses awareness of its past gradually loses its self. And so the political situation has brutally illuminated the ordinary metaphysical problem of forgetting that we face all the time, every day, without paying any attention. Politics unmasks the metaphysics of private life, private life unmasks the metaphysics of politics. (*Book* 234–35)

In short, as Kundera tells Roth, at the core of *The Book of Laughter and Forgetting* "is the story of totalitarianism, which deprives people of memory and thus retools them into a nation of children" (236).

*   *   *

Let me now return briefly to Nietzsche's and Yerushalmi's questions about how much we should remember and how much we should forget: "Given the need both to remember and to forget, where are the lines to be drawn? ... How much history do we require? What kind of history? What should we remember, what can we afford to forget, what must we forget?" Given the choice between too much memory and too little, Yerushalmi takes a very clear stance: "I will take my stand on the side of 'too much' rather than 'too little,' for my terror of forgetting is greater than my terror of having too much to remember." After all, he points out, we live in a world in which "it is no longer merely a question of the decay of collective memory and the declining consciousness of the past, but of the aggressive rape of whatever memory remains, the deliberate distortion of the historical record, the invention of mythological pasts in the service of the powers of darkness. Against the agents of oblivion, the shredders of documents, the assassins of memory, the revisers of encyclopedias, the conspirators of silence, against those who, in Kundera's wonderful image, can airbrush a man out of a photograph so that nothing is left of him but his hat—only the historian, with the austere passion for fact, proof, evidence, which are central to his vocation, can effectively stand guard" (Yerushalmi 116). This is a position, I would argue, fully endorsed by Milan Kundera, an unequivocal condemnation of national forgetting. James Joyce's stance, as I will go on to argue in Chap. 3, is more ambivalent and equivocal.

THE LIGHTNESS OF FORGETTING

If there ever was an individual character in modern fiction who desired the Kunderan/Nietzschean lightness of forgetting, it would be Ford Madox Ford's enigmatic (and variously interpreted) narrator in *The Good Soldier*, John Dowell. The novel is an epistemological case study of simultaneously knowing and not knowing (the very first paragraph features the verb "to know" seven different times), an exercise of detailed memory reconstruction and yet of amnesia at the same time:

You may well ask why I write. And yet my reasons are quite many. For it is not unusual in human beings who have witnessed the sack of a city or the falling to pieces of a people to desire to set down what they have witnessed for the benefit of unknown heirs or of generations infinitely remote; or, if you please, just to get the sight out of their heads. (Ford 7)

For Dowell, *writing*—setting one's story down on paper—involves at once the urge to remember and the simultaneous will to forget: as with the mixed purposes behind both monuments and mourning (according to Pierre Nora's argument about the function of monuments and memorials), the act of writing here is an attempt to remember ("to set down what they have witnessed for the benefit of unknown heirs or of generations infinitely remote") but also to make possible the act of forgetting ("or, if you please, just to get the sight out of their heads"). For writing and forgetting are linked: Writing becomes a way to reshape and interpret the past that one needs to forget.

Dowell himself, in recording the story, is struggling with his shattering and newfound knowledge that the happiness and stability he had experienced for over nine years—as one member of an elegant foursome (what he calls a "four-square minuet") consisting of two wealthy married couples, the Dowells and the Ashburnhams, spending much time traveling together in Europe—were in fact a sham, full of lies, deception, and adultery (including between his wife Florence and Edward Ashburnham). Dowell mourns his former state of blissful ignorance:

Permanence? Stability! I can't believe it's gone. I can't believe that that long, tranquil life, which was just stepping a minuet, vanished in four crashing days at the end of nine years and six weeks.... No, by god, it is false! It wasn't a minuet that we stepped; it was a prison—a prison full of screaming hysterics, tied down so that they might not outsound the rolling of our carriage wheels as we went along the shaded avenues of the Taunus Wald. (8–9)

The weight of such unwelcome knowledge conflicts with Dowell's desire for continued ignorance—to the degree that he poignantly questions which is more true: the shocking, actual facts he has lately learned, or the blissful happiness he had experienced during his long period of blindness and ignorance?

And yet I swear by the sacred name of my creator that it was true. It was true sunshine; the true music; the true plash of the fountains from the mouth of stone dolphins. For, if for me we were four people with the same tastes, with the same desires, acting—or, no, not acting—sitting here and there unanimously, isn't that the truth? If for nine years I have possessed a goodly apple that is rotten at the core and discover its rottennness only in nine years and six months less four days, isn't it true to say that for nine years I possessed a goodly apple? (9)

This is indeed a moving and compelling question. In other words: if I had lived for nine years believing something that gave me great happiness (and behaving accordingly), only to discover after nine years that it was all a sordid sham—isn't what I had experienced for nine years "true"? It is also, of course, a modernist question central to the "literary impressionism" of writers like Ford, Joseph Conrad, and Henry James: is not the individual perception, the subjective "impression," the only true and authentic measure of experience—in a world in which absolute Truth and reliable objectivity are increasingly under assault? Which is to say, in terms of memory: isn't the reconstructed memory, the creative act involved in memory work, the only true knowledge and identity we can have and keep? Is there anything more real than the internal/individual acts of "remembering" and memory-making—which are the mind's own way of exploring the "infinite possibilities" of memory through the acts of imagination and "writing"?

* * *

Dowell wonders how Florence could have carried on her infidelities for so long under his very nose, for "There doesn't seem to have been the actual time. It must have been when I was taking my baths, and my Swedish exercises, being manicured." (10); as he thinks back, though, he realizes that actually most of the time she was out of his sight, and he clearly had been blissfully ignorant. Dowell's desire is to return to that state of ignorance in which he happily followed a familiar and comfortable annual routine between the Dowells and Ashburnhams, a state of ignorance very much resembling the cattle Nietzsche claims that humans envy: "[T]hey do not know what is meant by yesterday or today, they leap about, eat, rest, digest, leap about again, and so from morn till night and from day to day, fettered to the moment and its pleasure or displeasure, and thus neither melancholy nor bored"—for "the man says 'I remember' and envies the animal, who at once forgets and for whom every moment really dies, sinks back into night and fog and is extinguished for ever" (Nietzsche 102). This ability to forget and attain oblivion and live in the present moment, unburdened by the nightmare which weighs on the brain of the living, is precisely what Dowell desires. Dowell is happiest when he feels "lightest," when he remembers and knows least; his is the desire to live without memory, without knowledge.

As a result, what he nostalgically remembers most are images of peace, security, and stability, encapsulated in the oft-revisited image of the white hotel dining room where he first met the Ashburnhams and the two couples first established that seemingly solid four-square structure upon which his happiness was dependent:

> I have *forgotten* the aspect of many things but I shall never *forget* the aspect of the dining-room of the Hotel Excelsior on that evening—and on so many other evenings. Whole castles have vanished from my memory, whole cities that I have never visited again, but that white room ... (Ford 26; my emphases)

Which is to say that what matters is what he chooses *not* to forget; one's past is only what one remembers or, more accurately, reconstructs. Similarly, his image of the Ashburnham's English estate of Branshaw Teleragh is a happy nostalgic vision of pastoral/feudal tranquility: "And then I had my first taste of English life. It was amazing ... I tell you it was the very spirit of peace" (22–23), obliviously unaware that the Ashburnham household (Edward, Nancy, and Leonora) were at that same moment all living a hellish life of psychological torture and suffering at Branshaw "in an agony ... such as passes the mind of man to imagine." Indeed, what Dowell most wants from life is what he had tried to achieve for his wife Florence, but which is, indeed, what he most desires for himself: the mindless, bovine peace of what he calls "a shock-proof world" (53).

Ironically enough, the whole story is in fact a prodigious feat of remembering, of setting down—in writing—a story by memory of every little fact, date, and detail[3]; but the narrative is also a testament to the burden of memory and the desire for oblivion. Once again, memory and forgetting are sides of the same coin, embedded and mutually implicated in the mind. Dowell actually remembers everything—but he might as well have forgotten everything, since, in his effort to maintain the bliss of ignorance, he refuses to put two and two together. Thus, he ignores all the hints and warnings that the Misses Hurlbird and Florence's uncle articulated in trying to dissuade him from marrying Florence (whom they know to be unchaste); he willingly buys into all of Florence's stories about her bad "heart," about her lover Jimmy, and so on. For it is in such ignorance that he is happiest: "Oh, God, they made me so happy that I doubt if even paradise, that shall smooth out all temporal wrongs, shall ever give me the like." Unfortunately, the postlapsarian Dowell who is now, retrospectively, remembering and narrating this "saddest story" is now burdened with the unhappy truth: "I suppose that, during all that time, I was a deceived husband and that Leonora was pimping for Edward" (75). The tragedy of Dowell's story is that human beings are unfortunately not like Nietzsche's cattle—and so he simply cannot now return to a state of ignorance and innocence, however much he may wish to forget. He can only try, if he can, to meaningfully reconstruct and reinterpret the past—that is, to write.

* * *

Modernist fiction seems obsessed with the forgetting and the rewriting of the past. F. Scott Fitzgerald's celebrated 1925 novel *The Great Gatsby* revolves around another central character—Jay Gatsby—who also wishes to slough off the nightmare of history and the burden of the past, a past he wants to erase altogether. He thus tries not only to forget the past but—in ways that Ford's Dowell seems unable—to actively construct new and different possibilities, by creating a new self and identity via a combination of Freud's "family romance`" and what I have called "amnesia fantasy":

> James Gatz—that was really, or at least legally, his name. He had changed it at the age of seventeen and at the specific moment that witnessed the beginning of his career …. I suppose he'd had the name ready for a long time, even then. His parents were shiftless and unsuccessful farm people—his imagination had never really accepted them as his parents at all. The truth was that Jay Gatsby of West Egg, Long Island, sprang from his Platonic conception of himself …. So he invented just the sort of Jay Gatsby that a seventeen-year-old boy would be likely to invent, and to this conception he was faithful to the end. (Fitzgerald 98)

The erasure of a clear, verifiable past—as with an amnesiac—allows for both the invented fantasy as well as for Aristotle's "room of infinite possibilities," thus fostering many rumors and speculations—such as: that "[Gatsby's] a nephew or a cousin of Kaiser Wilhelm's. That's where all his money comes from" (32); that "he killed a man once" (44); that "he was a German spy during the war" (44); that, conversely, "he was in the

American army during the war" (44); that "once he was an Oxford man" (49); that "he's a bootlegger"; that "One time he killed a man who had found out that he was nephew to Von Hindenburg and second cousin to the devil" (61); and so on, turning Gatsby into a source of unsubstantial speculation and fascination by the many who attend his parties but have no actual knowledge about their host. But Nick Carraway, the story's narrator, understands that Gatsby must have come from somewhere, for "young men didn't ... drift coolly out of nowhere and buy a palace on Long Island Sound" (49); in other words, Gatsby must have a real past and a real identity, however forgotten or erased.

But Gatsby tries to convince Nick: "I am the son of some wealthy people in the Middle West—all dead now. I was brought up in America but educated at Oxford, because all my ancestors have been educated there for many years. It's a family tradition .... My family all died and I came into a good deal of money .... After that I lived like a young rajah in all the capitals of Europe—Paris, Venice, Rome—collecting jewels, chiefly rubies, hunting big game, painting a little, things for myself only, and trying to *forget* something very sad that had happened to me long ago" (65–66; my emphasis). The irony in this invented "amnesia fantasy" is that the one bit of actual truth in this long list of romantically absurd fantasies is that very last line—that he had been "trying to *forget* something very sad that had happened to me long ago." That painful fact is, of course, that he had lost Daisy Buchanan because he was too poor to belong in her society and to marry her. In other words, the one truth in his invented story and identity is the one thing he most wishes he could forget—but cannot. In spite of his successful forgetting and erasure of the past, he is still the victim of too much memory, too much remembering. Indeed, one could speculate that the modernist novel's obsession with remembering/forgetting suggests and reflects an intense discomfort with the reality of one's culture (the burden of the past) and with one's personal present, repeatedly wishing to explore that room of infinite possibilities and alternate realities.

As a result, what Gatsby really wants is not so much to obliterate the past and the burden of memory at all, but actually to rewrite, to correct, the past: "He wanted nothing less of Daisy than that she should go to Tom and say: 'I never loved you.' After she had obliterated four years with that sentence they could decide upon the more practical measures to be taken. One of them was that, after she was free, they were to go back to Louisville and be married from her house—just as if it were five years ago" (109). In other words, he wants a chance to relive the past differently, to correct it, and do things the way he would have liked—now that he has a massive fortune by which to propose marriage to Daisy properly. Nick sensibly reminds Gatsby that "I wouldn't ask too much of her .... You can't repeat the past"; Gatsby's answer is both poignant and pathetic: "'Can't repeat the past?' he cried incredulously. 'Why of course you can!'" (110). In some ways, Gatsby's problem is that—in spite of the elaborate and very successful fantasy he has spun for himself—he simply can't forget the past; his "amnesia fantasy" and self-invention still don't allow him the comfort of actual forgetting, which is after all the presumed purpose of an "amnesia fantasy." Indeed, Gatsby's entire romantic drive is an over-whelming compulsion to repeat, and to fix, the past. Gatsby tries to create his own identity so that he can forget his past; what he doesn't understand is that identity is irrevocably tied to one's past. Gatsby's story is a stark lesson and reminder—as with the golden dream of America itself—that even if one can create a whole new world and self, the past will still con-tinue to haunt and drive one's psyche and identity: "So we beat on, boats against the current, borne back ceaselessly into the past" (180).

*   *   *

Wandering Amnesiacs and the Loss of Identity: Walker Percy and the South

The burden of memory and of the past continues to be an obsession with modern literature and with modernist writers, so fascinated as they are by issues of the self, individual identity, and the discontinuities and fissures in individual identity (so clearly obvious in protagonists like Ford's Dowell, Fitzgerald's Gatsby, Faulkner's Quentin Compson, Joyce's Stephen Dedalus, among many others). After all, one way of thinking about mem-ory is in terms of how a person conceives and imagines his or her own identity over time through the use of memories. What is the relationship between authenticity, identity, and memory? Scholarly discussions on the topic repeatedly invoke the philosopher John Locke, who stressed (in the words of Romantics scholar Frances Ferguson) "the importance of mem-ory for anchoring a sense of individual continuity over time" (see Rossington 70). In *An Essay Concerning Human Understanding* (1690), Locke attempted a "common-sense" definition of Identity: "[T]o find where *personal Identity* consists, we must consider what *Person* stands for; which,

I think, is a thinking intelligent Being, that has reason and reflection, and can consider it self as it self, the same thinking thing in different times and places" (quoted in Rossington 2). But modernist accounts of the self—whether in literature or in psychology—tend to focus on the discontinuity of the self and the breakdown of the unified sensibility or subject. As Joyce's Stephen Dedalus puts it, "Wait. Five months. Molecules all change. I am other I now" (*U* 9.205): so is an individual's identity, to use Stephen's formulations, a case of "I, I"—or is it a case of "I. I" (*U* 9.212)?—that is, is the "I" continuous or discontinuous? (Stephen adds, acknowledging the role of memory in identity, that "But I ... am I by memory because under everchanging forms"; *U* 9.208–9). Or as Bob Dylan puts it, "I wake and I'm one person, and when I go to sleep I know for certain I'm somebody else. I don't know *who* I am most of the time" (*Newsweek* October 6, 1997: 64). Similarly, contemporary thinkers and philosophers have qualified Locke's definition; for example, David Wiggins notes that "The hospitalized amnesiac or Nijinksy even at the last stage of madness are the same man and the same person." Thus, he suggests, we should "amend Locke" and realize that "Memory is not then irrelevant to personal identity, but the way it is relevant is simply that it is one highly important element among others" which "plays its part in determining the continuity principle for persons" (see Rossington 2–3). As Wiggins suggest, the physiological condition of amnesia is a useful way to think about such issues.

Indeed, amnesiacs are key scientific case studies for understanding the nature of individual identity and the role of memory-making in one's identity. There are many stories about amnesia and amnesiacs in popular literature, film, and television. But such stories are much rarer in more "serious" or canonical literature—and even rarer in real life. But the latter instances are particularly instructive. One such story is the enigma of Hannah Emily Upp's disappearance. I am going to detail briefly this real-life example—as a way to introduce the parallel case of an "actual" amnesiac in fiction, in Walker Percy's *The Last Gentleman*.

On March 1, 2009, the *New York Times* (*nytimes.com*) reported: "On Aug. 28 [2008], a Thursday, a 23-year-old schoolteacher from Hamilton Heights named Hannah Emily Upp went for a jog along Riverside Drive." Ms. Upp was a Spanish teacher at Thurgood Marshall Academy in Harlem, and it was the day before the start of a new school year. "That jog is the last thing that Ms. Upp says she remembers before the deckhands rescued her from the waters of New York Harbor on the morning of Tuesday, Sept. 16" (1). As Ms. Upp herself would later comment: "I went from going for a run to being in the ambulance. It was like 10 minutes had passed. But it was almost three weeks" (1).

What happened to her during those weeks is a matter of speculation and rumor: "It was as if the city had simply opened wide and swallowed her whole" (1)—though she was spotted on security cameras a few times at various locations in the city, clearly having traveled widely around the city before being rescued in the cold waters off Staten Island. But how did she get there—and how did she eat, and where did she sleep? She had left behind her wallet, her ID, and her cell phone: so "how did she survive for so long without money or any identification in one of the world's busiest and most complex cities?" (1)

Ms. Upp had graduated a year earlier from Bryn Mawr, and had taught Spanish for a year to seventh and eighth graders at Thurgood Marshall; she was also studying to get a Master's degree in education. She seemed to love her job. She clearly also loved to travel: in college she had spent a semester in Buenos Aires; she had visited Ghana, Poland, and Puerto Rico with the college choir; and she had traveled through Europe. During that past summer, she visited her brother in Japan (in the Navy); and visited a close friend from Bryn Mawr in New Delhi, where—even as a white woman who didn't speak Hindi—she managed to navigate the Old City by herself while her friend was at work.

After her amazing rescue from the waters of New York Harbor, Ms. Upp was treated for hypothermia and dehydration at Richmond University Medical Center in Staten Island. While there, she was diagnosed as having experienced "dissociative fugue," an extremely rare type of amnesia in which, out of the blue and for no apparent reason, victims lose all memories about their identity; the condition can last a few hours—or can last years. This is the form of amnesia so celebrated in popular film and fiction, and yet so rare in real life; few psychiatrists have ever witnessed a case of dissociative fugue, in which the victim is unable to recall his or her past at all. It is a condition also frequently characterized by sudden and unexpected travel. While victims of dissociative fugue continue to be able to perform everyday tasks (such as ordering a meal or using the Internet) without any problem, they lose the specific memories that have to do with their individual identity: "It's as if a whole set of information about one's self, our autobiography, goes off line," notes Dr. Richard Loewenstein, an expert on dissociative fugue and the medical director of the trauma program at Sheppard and Enoch Pratt Hospital in Baltimore.

Such an inability to recall one's past highlights the fragility of memory—and the degree to which our identity, our sense of who we are, depends on memory. As Dr. Loewenstein points out: "We tend to experience our identity as a thing, as if it's a constant. But it's a lot less stable and has less unity than we want to believe." Months later, Ms. Upp herself commented: "It's weird …. It's not your fault, but it's still somehow you. So it's definitely made me reconsider everything. Who was I before? Who was I then—is that part of me? Who am I now?" (2)

In recent years this condition has been popularly associated with the fictional secret agent Jason Bourne, the character at the center of a series of popular films and novels (by Robert Ludlum), portrayed by actor Matt Damon in the films. As the *New York Times* points out: "The Bourne character takes his name from Ansel Bourne, a Rhode Island preacher who suffered the earliest recorded case of the condition when he was en route to Providence in 1887. The preacher continued to Norristown, Pa., where he opened a store and lived with another family, until one day he 'woke up'" (3). Such travel is a typical characteristic of fugue states.[4] As Dr. Philip Coons, a psychiatrist and the author of a book on the topic, points out: "People have been known to not only travel across cities or countries, but also across continents. The explanation behind the fugue is that the person is running away from a bad situation, from a bad marriage or a bad financial situation" (3). Which is to say that the possible psychological causes behind the physiological symptoms of actual amnesia are, arguably, not at all unlike the motivations behind what I have been calling "amnesia fantasies"—that is, the urge to forget the burden of the past and to dispel the nightmare of history. So that the fugue is both a physiological symptom and a coping strategy. Indeed, even as she then attempted to restore her personal routines and start seeing her friends again so as to help reestablish her personal identity, Ms. Upp took a leave from her teaching job, wondering what caused her fugue state and whether it was significant "that she disappeared the day before school started": "There's a lot of room for self-doubt and confusion there," she notes. "And, well, I don't know. I certainly would never have intended to do that, but it makes you wonder" (7).

Like Hannah Upp, Will Barrett—the amnesiac protagonist of Walker Percy's novel *The Last Gentleman*—is prone to fugue states in which he wanders around the country, his life punctuated by long gaps (such as those three missing weeks of Ms. Upp's life): "Most of this young man's life was a gap. The summer before, he had fallen into a fugue state and wandered around northern Virginia for three weeks, where he sat sunk in thought on old battlegrounds, hardly aware of his own name" (*Last* 12). *The Last Gentleman,* set in the early Sixties, is the story of Williston Bibb Barrett, a young Southerner from the Mississippi Delta who had attended

Princeton (like a long line of males in his family) and is currently living in New York City, working as a night janitor and living at the YMCA. Barrett has a "nervous condition" which makes him prone to amnesiac fugues. In the novel, he meets the Vaughts, a wealthy family also from the Deep South who are in New York City so that their son Jamie, who is very ill, can receive the best medical attention available. Mr. Vaught (who, it turns out, knows Will's family back home) is very taken by Will—and invites him to return to the South with his family, offering Will a job as Jamie's companion. The novel focuses on the relationships between Will and the various members of the Vaught family—especially Mr. Vaught's daughter Kitty, whom Will falls in love with, and her brother Sutter, a brilliant but disgraced doctor from whom Will seeks guidance, both medical and philosophical, in his search for identity and for a stable self.

Walker Percy's novels are repeatedly concerned both with the medical condition of amnesia and with the burden of memory, especially—as with Faulkner and so many other Southern writers—the burden of the Southern past. A writer from Louisiana and also a medical doctor, Percy's shaping influences included William Faulkner, Roman Catholicism (he converted in 1947), Kierkegaard, Dostoevsky, and medicine. Percy's first novel, *The Moviegoer* (1962), had already previewed the attractions of the "amnesia fantasy" as a refuge from the burdens of memory; as that novel's main character Binx Bolling notes:

> It reminds me of a movie I saw last month .... The movie was about a man who lost his memory in an accident and as a result lost everything: his family, his friends, his money. He found himself a stranger in a strange city. He had to make a fresh start, find a new place to live, a new job, a new girl. It was supposed to be a tragedy, his losing all this, and he seemed to suffer a great deal. On the other hand, things were not so bad after all. In no time he found a very picturesque place to live, a houseboat on the river, and a very handsome girl, the local librarian. (*Moviegoer* 4)

The Last Gentleman's Will Barrett is similarly able to appreciate the "lightness" of the amnesiac condition: "And it was in fact very pleasant walking up Broadway instead of riding the subway every morning, one's mind wiped clean as a blackboard (not that it was necessary for him to try to 'put aside your usual worries,' since he forgot everything anyhow, worries included, unless he wrote them down)" (*Last* 46). This is the cattle-like condition that Nietzsche claimed humans envy. Indeed, *The Last Gentleman* begins with this epigraph (from Kierkegaard): "If a man cannot forget, he will never amount to much" (Soren Kierkegaard, *Either/Or*). Percy's novels are insistently concerned with an existential search for meaning in the modern world, especially in the contemporary South where the culture's traditional values and expectations seem to have been eroded, and life is thus plagued by daily ordinariness and existential "malaise": "Everydayness is the enemy. No search is possible. Perhaps there was a time when everydayness was not too strong and one could break its grip by brute strength. Now nothing breaks it—but disaster [or, as Percy's characters discover, amnesia]. Only once in my life was the grip of everydayness broken: when I lay bleeding in a ditch" (*Moviegoer* 145). In *The Last Gentleman*, amnesia is explored in a number of different ways—but especially in terms of how the individual burdens of memory and daily existence are tied—as in Kundera's and Joyce's novels—to a collective and "national" burden, in this case the Southern past. *The Last Gentleman* has to do with both versions of the "nightmare of history"—that is, with the burden of individual identity (in the forms of fugue states and amnesia fantasies), as well as with the drive toward a collective amnesia, the liberation of the past for a memory-haunted South.

At one point in the middle of the novel, Will asks Sutter Vaught: "Dr. Vaught, do you know what causes amnesia?" (219) Will's amnesia, the narrator informs us, "was now of this order: he forgot things he had seen before, but things he had heard of and not seen looked familiar. Old new things like fifty-year-old golf links where Bobby Jones played once were haunted by memory" (188); whatever the causes of Will's amnesia, Percy's novel seems repeatedly to suggest that they have to do with the hauntings of memory and the past. While the specific psychological causes of his neurological condition are not known, the symptoms are by now familiar to Will: "To be specific, he had now a nervous condition and suffered spells of amnesia and even between times did not quite know what was what. Much of the time he was like a man who had just crawled out of a bombed building. Everything looked strange"; however, like Binx in *The Moviegoer*, Will realizes that "Such a predicament, however, is not altogether a bad thing. Like the sole survivor of a bombed building, he had no secondhand opinions and he could see things afresh" (11).

His condition is marked by a recurrence of amnesiac fugues (for example, page 22: "It was shortly after the weekend at Bear Mountain that he lapsed into a fugue state which was worse than the last"), during which he wanders and travels around the country—as is frequently the case with amnesiacs during fugue states. During such times, we are told, "He would lapse into an unproductive and solitary life. He took to wandering. He had a way of turning up at unlikely places such as a bakery in Cincinnati or a greenhouse in Memphis, where he might work for several weeks assaulted by the *deja vus* of hot growing green plants" (12). These wanderings give the novel a striking and strangely picaresque flavor, generically and textually reproducing the experience of fugue wandering. Previously, we are told, Barrett had been drafted and had "served two years in the United States Army, where he took a large number of courses in electronics and from which he was honorably and medically discharged when he was discovered totally amnesic and wandering about the Shenandoah Valley between Cross Keys and Port Republic, sites of notable victories of General Stonewall Jackson" (17–18). And "the summer before, he had fallen into a fugue state and wandered around northern Virginia for three weeks, where he sat sunk in thought on old battlegrounds, hardly aware of his own name" (12). Indeed, as these last two quotations suggest, somehow Will's fugue states seem repeatedly to have to do with the Civil War and with a traumatic Southern past haunted by loss, defeat, and racial strife—the South's own "nightmare of history." Will Barrett's amnesia might be characterized as an attempt to awake from the nightmare of Southern history by attempting—but being unable—to erase the past altogether.

Furthermore, Percy's protagonists struggle with the attempt to find meaning in a modern world with uncertain values and traditions, and thus to learn how to act honorably and meaningfully. Like Binx in *The Moviegoer*, Will Barrett searches for definition, for clear-cut situations. Such imposed definition could transcend, and break the grip of, the "malaise" of ordinary, everyday life and all of its infinite, dull possibilities. Such clear-cut and imposed definition would allow one to act and react in clear-cut ways, allowing oneself to know who one is and what role one has to play. As Barrett puts it:

> Luck would be this: if he saw her [his beloved Kitty] snatch a purse, flee into the park [Central Park] pursued by cops. Then he would know something and could do something. He could hide her in a rocky den he had discovered in a wild section of the park. He would bring her food and they would sit and talk until nightfall, when they could slip out of the city and go home to Alabama. Such a turn of events was unlikely, however. (64)

The existential dilemma for Barrett (indeed, for all of us) lies in steering a real and actual course through the sea of infinite possibilities that life presents: "For until this moment he had lived in a state of pure possibility, not knowing what sort of a man he was or what he must do, and supposing therefore that he must be all men and do everything .... Lucky is the man who does not secretly believe that every possibility is open to him" (4). As with Binx and Kate in *The Moviegoer*, Barrett's struggle is between one's desire to be able to conform to a defined "good-soldier" code and to the traditions of the old South, and the necessity to cope in a modern world where there are no codes and defined modes of behavior, where every course is equally possible:

> Like many young men in the South, he became overly subtle and had trouble ruling out the possible .... Southerners have trouble ruling out the possible. What happens to a man to whom all things seem possible and every course of action open? Nothing of course. Except war. If a man lives in the sphere of the possible and waits for something to happen, what he is waiting for is war—or the end of the world. That is why Southerners like to fight and make good soldiers. In war the possible becomes actual through no doing of one's own. (10)

In a war, one presumably knows how to act and what one has to do. In *The Moviegoer*, Binx had envied his father for having been given the luxury of war (World War II), and thus a solution to the existential dilemma—since his father had managed to escape the malaise of daily life and to play out a version of the escapist "amnesia fantasy" by going to war (and dying) in World War II: "He had found a way to do both: to please them and please himself. To leave. To do what he wanted to do and save old England doing it. And perhaps even carry off the grandest coup of all: to die. To win the big prize for them and for himself (but not even he dreamed he would succeed not only in dying but in dying in Crete in the wine dark sea)" (*Moviegoer* 157).

When Will Barrett does find himself, later in the novel, back in the South, it is both a reassuring and a disconcerting experience. On the one hand, he understands better now how to behave in the South: "In the space of seconds he changed from a Southerner in the North, an amiable person who wears the badge of his origin in a faint burlesque of itself, to a Southerner in the South, a skillful player of an old play who knows his cues and waits smiling in the wings" (*Last* 55). For in the South interactions and conversations involve "ten assumptions shared and a common stance of rhetoric and whole shared set of special ironies and opposites. He was home" (161). But, on the other hand, it is also in the South that he simply cannot escape the nightmare of history, for—as with

Joyce's characters on the streets of Dublin—everywhere he runs into reminders of it. For example, there is Mr. Vaught's "Confederate Chevrolet agency, the second largest in the world. Dozens of salesmen in Reb-colonel hats and red walking canes threaded their way between handsome Biscaynes and sporty Corvettes" (261).

A "Confederate" Chevrolet dealership in which salesmen wear Reb-colonel hats is just one of the many reminders he encounters of the South's troubled history. As I mentioned earlier, somehow Barrett's fugue states seem repeatedly connected with the Civil War and with the Southern past—as when he was "discovered totally amnesic and wandering about the Shenandoah Valley between Cross Keys and Port Republic, sites of notable victories of General Stonewall Jackson" (17–18) or when "the summer before, he had fallen into a fugue state and wandered around northern Virginia for three weeks, where he sat sunk in thought on old battlegrounds, hardly aware of his own name" (12). Now, back in the South with the Vaughts, Barrett starts reading "Freeman's *R. E. Lee*" and imagining himself "correcting the horrific Confederate foul-ups, in this case the foul-up before Sharpsburg when Lee's battle orders had been found by a Union sergeant, the paper wrapped around three cigars and lying in a ditch in Maryland": Barrett fantasizes that "I'll pick it up before he gets there" (225–226). Barrett wishes to rewrite Civil War history—presumably so that the South might have won the war, and his "nightmare of history" might not be so acute and traumatic.[5]

Will, Jamie, and Kitty now all decide to enroll at the "university forty miles away," and "two weeks later [Will] and Jamie had pledged Phi Nu" while Kitty had become a Chi Omega (191). The University itself becomes, for Will, another significant site representing the nightmare of Southern history, for not only is its football team named the "Colonels," but it is— as we learn—about to witness a serious Civil Rights incident, for there were "rumors of a Negro student coming on campus next week" (227). In the novel the university itself is never actually named, but it is clearly a major football power: "The Tennessee game is tomorrow," Kitty reports— for "Overnight she had turned into a fierce partisan for the Colonels, who were now ranked number two in the United States" while "Tennessee is number four" (248). Presumably, then, this fictional university (whose team is the "Colonels") is modeled on either Ole Miss (the Rebels) or Alabama (the Crimson Tide), the two big Southern football powers in the Delta during the Sixties. It was at Ole Miss—the University of Mississippi at Oxford (also Faulkner's hometown), whose mascot is "Colonel Reb"— that, in September 1962, James Meredith tried to enroll as the first black student in the school's history—triggering resistance from the University, the state, and the governor (Ross Barnett), and forcing President John F. Kennedy to order federal marshals to campus to make sure that Meredith could enroll safely. While the President addressed the nation that night in a live television speech about the volatile situation, violence broke out on the campus, leading to federal troops descending on Oxford to stop the riots, which killed two people and injured over 300. And it was at the University of Alabama that, a few months later in June 1963, two black students, Vivian Malone and James Hood, attempted to register—even as Governor George Wallace (who had been elected on the slogan "Segregation now, segregation tomorrow, segregation forever"), despite a federal court order barring any state interference, appointed himself University registrar and tried to block the students from registering by standing in the doorway of the administration building. President Kennedy then sent in a federalized National Guard, who escorted the students to campus and to a successful registration.

At this point in the novel, Will Barrett finds himself at the bar one evening with a bunch of classmates from the University who "were talking about politics and the Negro, who was now rumored to be headed for the campus this weekend" (266). One of the young men, Lamar Thigpen, asks: "Do yall know the difference between a nigger and an ape?" This conversation so unsettles Barrett—"who was so mystified by white and black alike that he could not allow himself the luxury of hatred"—that he takes his own pulse: "'I'm not at all well,' he said to himself" (266). When Sutter notices his distress and asks him what the matter is, we have this revealing exchange:

> "I think my nervous condition is worse. I feel my memory slipping."
> "What was that book you were reading earlier?"
> "Freeman's *R. E. Lee*."
> "Are you still strongly affected by the Civil War?"
> "Not as strongly as I used to be."
> "How strongly was that?"

Will then reveals a story from his college days:

> When I was at Princeton, I blew up a Union monument. It was only a plaque hidden in the weeds behind the chemistry building, presented by the class of 1885 in memory of those who made the supreme sacrifice to suppress the infamous rebellion, or something like that. It offended me. I synthesized a

liter of trinitrotoluene [TNT] in the chemistry lab and blew it up one
Saturday afternoon. But no one ever knew what had been blown up. It
seemed I was the only one who knew the monument was there. It was
thought to be a Harvard prank. (267)

Sutter, a brilliant medical doctor and diagnostician, realizes that Barrett's
neurological conditions may be related to his feelings about the South,
and now asks him: "Are your nationalistic feelings strongest before the
onset of your amnesia?" "Perhaps they are," Barrett replies (267). Here,
the individual urge to forget merges with a cultural/regional need to
come to terms with a traumatic past—in a symbolic act of subaltern opposition to the ruling powers, blowing up a Union monument.[6]

Unable to sleep that night, Barrett feels himself slipping into a fugue,
and "by three o'clock in the morning he was worse off than at any time
since Eisenhower was President when he had worked three months for a
florist in Cincinnati, assaulted by the tremendous *deja vus* of hot green
growing things" (269). He goes to seek help from Sutter ("I have reason
to believe I am going into a fugue .... I thought you might be able to help
me"). It is in this very hazy and tenuous condition that, a couple of days
later, he is driving Kitty to campus the evening after the big game with
Tennessee, to pick up Kitty's books. As they arrive, Barrett realizes that
"Something was wrong .... There were flat popping noises .... In the next
block an old car stopped and three men got out carrying shotguns and
dove straight into the woods. They were not students. They looked like
the men who hang around service stations in south Jackson" (288). As he
and Kitty walk onto campus to get their books, Will sees dark figures running wildly, and then a girl walks up to him: "'He's here,' she sobbed ....
'Kill him! Kill him! Kill him!'" (288) While the hazy Barrett has no idea
what she is referring to, it is clear to the reader that the "Negro" student
is now on campus and that the situation had sparked violent disturbances.
At this point, "at the Confederate monument a group of students ran
toward [Barrett] in ragged single file. Then he saw why. They were carrying a long flagstaff. The flag was furled" (288). As they swing the flagstaff
around, the bewildered Barrett is unable to get out of the way—and he is
struck on the head by the flagstaff and knocked unconscious at the base of
the Confederate monument. By the time Barrett comes to hours later,
"the streets were littered with broken glass" and "one automobile had
been set afire and burned to a cinder" even as army trucks and police cars
and sirens were everywhere. But Barrett is in a total fugue now: "What is

this place? Where am I going?–he asked himself" (292); "he had forgotten Kitty and left her at the university and now remembered nothing more than that he had forgotten .... strangely he had forgotten the Vaughts and even the Y.M.C.A. and remembered Princeton" (294).

It is both hilariously and poignantly ironic—and symbolically appropriate—that Barrett is knocked unconscious and into a total fugue state by what is presumably the rebel flag of the Confederacy,[7] that *bête noire* of his own personal, family, and national history. For Barrett's fugues are caused by the traumas of Southern racial history, the burden of a collective past he simply can't slough off. As we learn a little later (when Will recollects a traumatic night from his boyhood), Will's father had shot and killed himself (pages 329–334): this incident was itself a representative Southern racial trauma, for his father, a liberal lawyer, had defended the rights of black folks, and as a consequence had received death threats from his fellow white Southerners. Will's own family history is thus deeply intertwined with that of the South, so that Will Barrett's amnesia is at once both a symptom and a coping mechanism. He becomes, in Percy's novel, an embodiment of the need to forget the burden of one's individual and family history—as well as the desire to forget the nightmare of a collective past, a shared Southern history of loss, defeat, racism, and shame. As Sutter Vaught writes in his journal: "Look Barrett, your trouble is due not to a disorder of your organism but to the human condition .... That is to say, your amnesia is not a symptom" (354). In other words, amnesia and the will to forget may well be a logical and necessary response to a widespread, contemporary human condition.

NOTES

1. The previous page is adapted from material in Chap. 2 of Cheng, *Shakespeare and Joyce: A Study of "Finnegans Wake."*
2. Similarly, the Chinese government has been trying, disturbingly successfully, to erase any memories and evidence of the 1989 massacre in Tiananmen Square. (See, for example, Helen Gao, "Forgetting Tiananmen" in the *New York Times*, June 4, 2014, page A21.)
3. See Cheng's "A Chronology of *The Good Soldier*" for all these factual dates and details.
4. For example, in August 2012, a man from North Carolina was found having traveled over 1000 miles in just such an amnesiac fugue:

   Man with amnesia travels 1,000 miles: Hugh Armstrong says he hitchhiked and walked 1,000 miles south from New Hampshire, even doing odd jobs along the way, without knowing who he was. But he knew his age and thought he might know someone in Asheville. Armstrong, 72, hadn't been able to remember his name since he fell into a ravine while walking near New Hampshire's Stinson Lake on July 25. A sheriff's deputy found him walking on U.S. 70 at 1:30 a.m. Saturday and identified him as a missing person by the initials on his wedding band. (*Salt Lake Tribune* August 12, 2012: A2)

5. This might be part of the attraction and motivation for Civil War "reenactors" today. See Tony Horwitz, *Confederates in the Attic: Dispatches from the Unfinished Civil War.*
6. See also Chaps. 4 and 6 of this study, on monuments and memory in both Ireland and the American South.
7. See also Chap. 6 of this study, on this at-once cherished and hated symbol of the antebellum, slaveholding South.

WORKS CITED

Casey, Edward S. *Remembering: A Phenomenological Study.* Second Edition. Bloomington: Indiana University Press, 2000.

Cheng, Vincent J. *Shakespeare and Joyce: A Study of "Finnegans Wake."* University Park: Penn State University Press, 1984.

———. *Joyce, Race, and Empire.* Cambridge: Cambridge University Press, 1995.

———. "A Chronology of *The Good Soldier*." In Ford, Ford Madox, *The Good Soldier.* Ed. Martin Stannard. New York: Norton Critical Edition, 2012. 391–395.

Faulkner, William. *Requiem for a Nun.* New York: Vintage, 1951.

Fitzgerald, F. Scott. *The Great Gatsby.* New York: Scribner, 1925, 2004.

Ford, Ford Madox. *The Good Soldier: A Tale of Passion.* New York: Vintage International, 1989.

Gao, Helen. "Forgetting Tiananmen." *New York Times*, June 4, 2014, page A21.

Horwitz, Tony. *Confederates in the Attic: Dispatches from the Unfinished Civil War.* New York: Vintage, 1999.

Joyce, James. *Ulysses.* Eds. Hans Walter Gabler et al. New York: Vintage, 1986.

Kundera, Milan. *The Book of Laughter and Forgetting.* Trans. Michael Henry Heim. New York: Penguin, 1981.

———. *The Unbearable Lightness of Being.* Trans. Michael Henry Heim. New York: Harper & Row, 1985.

Marx, Karl. From *The Eighteenth Brumaire of Louis Bonaparte.* In Rossington and Whitehead 97–101.

Nietzsche, Friedrich. *From* "On the Uses and Disadvantages of History for Life." In Rossington and Whitehead 102–108.

Nora, Pierre. *Les lieux de mémoire*, vol. I. Paris: Editions Gallimard, 1997.

Percy, Walker. *The Moviegoer.* New York: Noonday, 1961, 1967.

————. *The Last Gentleman*. New York: Farrar, Straus, and Giroux, 1966.

Renan, Ernest. "What Is a Nation?" Trans. Martin Thom. In Homi K. Bhabha, ed., *Nation and Narration*. 8–22.

Rossington, Michael and Anne Whitehead, editors. *Theories of Memory: A Reader.* Baltimore: Johns Hopkins University Press, 2007.

Whitehead, Anne. *Memory.* New York: Routledge, 2009.

Yerushalmi, Yosef Hayim. *Zakhor: Jewish History and Jewish Memory.* New York: Schocken Books, 1989.

CHAPTER 3

The Will to Forget: Nation and Forgetting in *Ulysses*

Friedrich Nietzsche has argued, as we have seen, that both remembering and willed/active forgetting—what Nietzsche calls the "historical" and the "unhistorical"—are necessary to the health and happiness of an individual, as well as of a nation: "Cheerfulness, the good conscience, the joyful deed, confidence in the future—all of them depend, in the case of the individual as of a nation, … on one's being just as able to forget at the right time as to remember at the right time; on the possession of a powerful instinct for sensing when it is necessary to feel historically and when unhistorically. This, precisely, is the proposition the reader is invited to meditate upon: *the unhistorical and the historical are necessarily in equal measure for the health of an individual, of a people and of a culture"* (104; Nietzsche's emphases).

In approaching Joyce's *Ulysses*—as a literary case study of such dynamics—I want to turn first to Ernest Renan, the nineteenth-century French historian and philosopher, and (along with Nietzsche) one of the few staunch advocates of forgetting—or at least of the necessity of forgetting, perhaps even of the collective will and urge to forget. This takes place in Renan's important and influential 1882 lecture "*Qu'est-ce qu'une nation?*" ("What Is a Nation?"). Joyce, we know, read and admired Renan's work: Stephen Daedalus cites Renan three separate times in *Stephen Hero* (175, 189, 190), the unpublished prototype for *A Portrait of the Artist as a Young Man*; Renan is mentioned in the "Scylla and Charybdis" episode

© The Author(s) 2018
V. J. Cheng, *Amnesia and the Nation*, New Directions in Irish and Irish American Literature, https://doi.org/10.1007/978-3-319-71818-7_3

of *Ulysses* (*U* 9.765–57); and Joyce, living in France, had visited Renan's birthplace (at Tréguier in Brittany; Ellmann II, 567). Joyce was clearly familiar with a number of Renan's well-known works—including, I would suggest, "What Is a Nation?" Indeed, there are a number of passages in Joyce's own essay "Ireland, Isle of Saints and Sages" that seem almost direct echoes of passages and arguments in Renan's essay. And, of course, in the "Cyclops" episode of *Ulysses* Leopold Bloom is asked to define what a nation is ("do you know what a nation means?" *U* 12.1419), echoing Renan's famous question and title.

"What Is a Nation?" has been a foundational text for contemporary studies and understandings of nationalism and national identity.[1] Whereas previous scholars had tried to define the nation by criteria such as a race or an ethnic group having shared characteristics, Renan—in a revolutionary departure—defined it by the desire of a people to live together, which he articulated in his well-known phrase, *avoir fait de grandes choses ensemble, vouloir en faire encore* ("to have performed great deeds together, to wish to perform still more"). Renan writes:

> A nation is a soul, a spiritual principle. Two things, which in truth are but one, constitute this soul or spiritual principle. One lies in the past, one in the present. One is the possession in common of a rich legacy of memories; the other is present-day consent, the desire to live together, the will to perpetuate the value of the heritage that one has received in an undivided form …. To have common glories in the past and to have a common will in the present; to have performed great deeds together, to wish to perform still more—these are the essential conditions for being a people. (Renan 19)

And what is required to solidify this desire to live together as a nation, Renan argues, is the process of forgetting. For purposes of a nation's collective well-being, some things are better forgotten:

> Forgetting, I would even go so far as to say historical error, is a crucial factor in the creation of a nation, which is why progress in historical studies often constitutes a danger for [the principle of] nationality. Indeed, historical enquiry brings to light deeds of violence which took place at the origin of all political formations, even those whose consequences have been altogether beneficial. Unity is always effected by means of brutality; the union of northern France with the Midi was the result of massacres and terror lasting for the best part of a century. (11)

If unity is a forced condition, achieved through brutality, then the maintenance of that unity requires a shared willingness to forget the brutal past. Indeed, Renan notes that the ability of a nation's people to feel things in common depends on the erasing of memories of discord and violence against each other: "Yet the essence of a nation is that all individuals have many things in common; and also that they have forgotten many things. No French citizen knows whether he is a Burgundian, an Alan, a Taifale, or a Visigoth, yet every French citizen has to have forgotten the massacre of Sa[i]nt Bartholomew, or the massacres that took place in the Midi in the thirteenth century" (11; many thousands of Huguenots were massacred in Paris on Saint Bartholomew's Day, August 24, 1572—a historical event Joyce also refers to twice in *Ulysses*, 8.622–24 and 15.2385).

It is easy to think of many examples in support of Renan's assertion—from the *Aeneid*'s suggestion of how forgetting past rancors allowed for the creation of the state of Rome to the Troubles in Northern Ireland, whose continuation were incited and facilitated for decades by the annual Orange marches by Protestants through Catholic neighborhoods each July, constantly *reminding* Catholics of (that is to say, refusing to allow them to forget) their status as colonial subjects. It is only when both sides are willing to begin the process of forgetting past atrocities that a peace process becomes possible. As Renan puts it, "It is good for everyone to know how to forget" (16).

Benedict Anderson, in his chapter "Memory and Forgetting" in *Imagined Communities*, extends Renan's argument about national forgetting by noting the discursive process by which such forgetting takes place—in which the memory of brutal massacre and enmity is replaced by a revisionist story of family discord, a process of reimaging such divisive memories as disagreements taking place, as it were, "all in the family." He cites Renan's argument about the St. Bartholomew massacre as an example of such a "construction of national genealogies":

> The effect of this tropology is to figure episodes in the colossal religious conflicts of mediaeval and early modern Europe as reassuringly fratricidal wars between—who else—*fellow Frenchmen* .... we become aware of a systematic historiographical campaign, deployed by the state mainly through the state's school system, to "remind" every young Frenchwoman and Frenchman of a series of antique slaughters which are now inscribed as "family history." (Anderson 200-01)

Anderson goes on to cite the example of how Americans are constantly taught to remember/forget the War Between the States as a "civil" war between "brothers" rather than as one between what were, at least for a while, two sovereign states. Of the genealogy of English national identity, Anderson writes:

> English history textbooks offer the diverting spectacle of a great Founding Father whom every schoolchild is taught to call William the Conqueror. The same child is not informed that William spoke no English, indeed could not have done so, since the English language did not exist in his epoch; nor is he or she told "Conqueror of what?" For the only intelligible modern answer would have to be "Conqueror of the English," which would turn the old Norman predator into a more successful precursor of Napoleon and Hitler. Hence "the Conqueror" operates as the same kind of ellipsis [or we might say *amnesia*] as "la Saint-Barthelemy" [the Saint Bartholomew massacre], to remind one of something which it is immediately obligatory to forget. Norman William and Saxon Harold thus meet on the battlefield of Hastings, if not as dancing partners, at least as brothers. (201)

It's a family affair. Perhaps in future generations the Troubles in Northern Ireland will also be thus retrospectively represented and reimagined as a fraternal spat within the Irish family, allowing both sides to forget their deep enmity and thus move on to a sense of collective and national commonality. This is how, Anderson suggests, a people constructs a national narrative and identity: "All profound changes in consciousness, by their very nature, bring with them characteristic amnesias. Out of such oblivions, in specific historical circumstances, spring narratives .... But, to serve the narrative purpose, these violent deaths must be remembered/forgotten as 'our own'" (204, 206).

Yet the question arises whether such collective amnesia can be permanent, or whether—as with repressed memories in trauma victims—there will at some point emerge a return of the repressed. Indeed, one could well think of the more recent cycles of genocidal violence during the 1990s in what was formerly Yugoslavia as the result of a return/resurfacing (or active disinterment) of repressed collective memories of ethnic conflicts and hatreds between Serbs, Croats, and Bosnians originating centuries earlier, all of which had been "forgotten" for a few decades (at least since the brutal ethnic strifes in the region during the 1940s) in the process of unifying these different groups under the national identity of the Yugoslav Federation. Renan himself was conscious of such a threat, and his warning almost seems now prescient in light of recent genocides in places like Serbia, Croatia, and Rwanda:

> Be on your guard, for this ethnographic politics is in no way a stable thing and, if today you use it against others, tomorrow you may see it turned against yourselves. Can you be sure that the Germans, who have raised the banner of ethnography so high, will not see the Slavs in their turn analyse the names of villages in Saxony and Lusatia, search for any traces of the Wiltzes or of the Obotrites, and demand recompense for the massacres and the wholesale enslavements that the Ottoss inflicted upon their ancestors? It is good for everyone to know how to forget. (Renan 15–16)

*   *   *

Joyce's texts are frequently concerned with the dynamics of forgetting, as well as with the contrasting struggle to hold on to "the memory of the past." For example, in the last lines of "The Boarding House" we are told that Polly Mooney found "her memories gradually giving place to hopes and visions of the future" which were "so intricate that she no longer saw the white pillows on which her gaze was fixed or remembered that she was waiting for anything." It is only when her mother interrupts her reverie and calls her to come downstairs because "Mr Doran wants to speak to you" that "[t]hen she remembered what she had been waiting for" (*D* 68–69). What she was waiting for, which she had conveniently forgotten, was of course a marriage proposal from Mr. Doran, the result of her and her mother's unspoken complicity in the dynamics of sexual entrapment. But the reader knows that Polly, in her "wise innocence" (64), was conscious all along of these dynamics. But for the sake of her own psychic health and self-respect, Polly needs to "remember to forget"—or at least temporarily suppress—this unpleasant reality, so that, when the call comes, it can *almost* (but not quite) seem like a pleasant surprise.

There are in Joyce's works many such interesting cases of the psychological maneuvers and self-deceptions involved in the processes of remembering and forgetting: Maria's need to forget/repress details (such as the discussions at the cake shop with the shopgirl, and on the tram with the "colonel-looking gentleman") that remind her of her own unmarriageable status (see Margot Norris, "Narration"); Gretta Conroy's romantic and nostalgic memories of Michael Furey in "The Dead"; and so on. In *Ulysses*, everyone is forgetful: Stephen, for example, remembers that it has now been twice that he has forgotten to take the library slips (3.407); Bloom forgets to take his latchkey with him, and forgets to pick up the lotion Molly asked for (5.468, 11.940, 17.79, 18.460); and so on. Each one of them tries to think of ways to remember better (see also John Rickard's study of "The Mnemotechnics of *Ulysses*" in *Joyce's Book of Memory*).

But these are cases of individual forgetfulness. In this chapter I want first to focus briefly on three passages in *Ulysses* in which individual forgetting becomes (as in Kundera's and Percy's novels) symptomatic of, or connected to, collective forgetting—to national, cultural, and historical forgetting.

*   *   *

The second chapter of *Ulysses*, the "Nestor" episode, an episode Joyce designated as concerning "History," begins with a history lesson:

> —You, Cochrane, what city sent for him?
> —Tarentum, sir.
> —Very good. Well?
> —There was a battle, sir.
> —Very good. Where?
>   The boy's blank face asked the blank window. (*U* 2.1–6)

Stephen's young student Cochrane is only partially able to recall the history of Pyrrhus's war against the Romans on behalf of the Tarentines. Tarentum was a minor Greek colony, fighting against the powerful Romans; thus, the story/history Stephen is asking his class to remember is one of a battle against empire. But history, Stephen's interior thoughts suggest, is "[f]abled by the daughters of memory" (*U* 2.7)—for memory, like Cochrane, has a hard time remembering facts and details and instead imagines "fables" or allegories:

> —I forget the place, sir. 279 B.C.
> —Asculum, Stephen said, glancing at the name and date in the gorescarred book.
> —Yes, sir. And he said: *Another victory like that and we are done for.*
>   That phrase the world had remembered. A dull ease of the mind. From a hill above a corpsestrewn plain a general speaking to his officers ....
> (*U* 2.11–17)

What gets remembered, Stephen realizes, is discourse—in this case, the famous phrase attributed to Pyrrhus: *Another victory like that and we are done for.* What gets forgotten and repressed (in the distillation of a battle into a single phrase the world still remembers) are the actual and material circumstances at Asculum that led to Pyrrhus's comment in the first place, the facts behind the logic of a "Pyrrhic victory": that is, the tremendous human slaughter and bloodshed that made another such victory unthinkable, even for the victors. Thus, Stephen's history book is "gorescarred" in more ways than one, as it tells the story of a general (Pyrrhus) speaking to his officers above a "corpsestrewn" plain—while the world remembers only that catchy phrase, exercising "a dull ease of the mind." The discursive, collective memory whitewashes and simplifies painful or unpleasant historical details: what is forgotten (in favor of discourse) are gore and death.

Although Stephen's young Irish students might be expected to identify with a battle fought by a small colony against a powerful empire, "For them, too," Stephen thinks, "history was a tale like any other too often heard, their land a pawnshop" (*U* 2.46–47). It is perhaps easier to want to forget, to exercise the "dull ease of the mind." Stephen himself, however, like Luria's mnemonist, sees too much, and cannot forget; for him history "is a nightmare from which I am trying to awake" (*U* 2.377). Even the game of hockey the students go on to play reminds Stephen of the ugly dynamics embodied in such play which mimics (and sometimes enacts) actual violence:

> Again: a goal. I am among them, among their battling bodies in a medley, the joust of life .... Jousts. Time shocked rebounds, shock by shock. Jousts, slush and uproar of battles, the frozen deathspew of the slain, a shot of spearspikes baited with men's bloodied guts. (*U* 2.314–18)

The game itself is imaged by Stephen as training and preparation for battle and for killing (as in the well-known phrase about Waterloo being won on the "playing fields of Eton," as training grounds for a male ideology and tradition of blood and warfare), as the sounds of sticks clashing and jousting for rebounds are but preludes to the gorescarred and corpsestrewn plains of war that await these young boys when they grow up: "Time shocked rebounds, shock by shock. Jousts, slush and uproar of battles, the frozen deathspew of the slain, a shout of spearspikes baited with men's bloodied guts." Again, what we forget and repress is blood and corpses;

what we remember are stories and witty phrases ("another victory like that …" and "the playing fields of Eton"), the very discursive products that elide the gorescarred and corpsestrewn plains behind them. So also contemporary, discursive euphemisms like "friendly fire" and "collateral damage" sanitize and mask the reality that what we are really talking about is blood and death.

Renan argues that national identity and unity depend on collective acts of forgetting. For a nation, such unity is obviously desirable. One might note that, for an empire, such unity is even more desirable (but perhaps harder to achieve), for—from the imperialist's standpoint—it is important for a colony and its colonial subjects to forget the history of bloody conquest (to bury the blood-stained hatchet, as it were) if they are to reimagine their own collective identity and future as a happy part of the empire. But for Stephen, a member of the conquered race, history is not so easily forgotten or repressed. In other words, it is the victors who would most want to forget past atrocities; it is the losers who most need to not forget. It is easier for Stephen's students, affluent and comfortable under the empire—"Welloff people, proud that their eldest son was in the navy," living in exclusive and expensive neighborhoods such as the "Vico road, Dalkey" and sending their boys to an expensive school ("aware of the fees their papas pay") run by an Ulsterman—it is easier for them to forget the troubled past of Ireland, "a tale like any other too often heard," than for a poor Catholic like Stephen obsessed with the nightmare of history (*U* 2.24–47).

And no one in *Ulysses* forgets more easily than Garrett Deasy, the headmaster and Stephen's boss at the school. A Protestant and an Ulsterman, a member of the Anglo-Irish Ascendancy ruling Ireland, Deasy, ironically, accuses Stephen of forgetfulness:

—You think me an old fogey and an old tory …. I saw three generations since O'Connell's time. I remember the famine in '46. Do you know that the orange lodges agitated for repeal of the union twenty years before O'Connell did or before the prelates of your communion denounced him as a demagogue? You fenians forget some things. (*U* 2.268–72)

But it is Deasy himself who repeatedly forgets or misremembers or distorts historical facts—whether it is in quoting Shakespeare's *Put but money in thy purse* (Iago, Stephen reminds him); in claiming that a French Celt came up with the line "That on [the British] empire the sun never sets";

or that Catholic prelates "denounced" Daniel O'Connell (*U* 2.239–40, 248–49, 271–72). And he is certainly wrong in his self-satisfied announcement to Stephen that "Ireland, they say, has the honour of being the only country which never persecuted the Jews .... And do you know why? ... Because she never let them in" (*U* 2.437–42).

Forgetting is a convenient luxury of the winners. It is clearly beneficial to the unity of a sovereign state or empire for its subjects to be able to forget the history of bloody conquest if they are to partake in a collective identity as members of such sovereignty. For the recalcitrant members of a subject colony resisting imperial rule, however, forgetting is, for that same reason, precisely *not* desirable: it is the pre-conquest past, the traditional native culture, that one must hold on to, that one must try to reclaim, must try to still remember Zion by the rivers of Babylon, all the while not allowing oneself to be contaminated by the attractions of empire, by the "fleshpots of Egypt," as it were.

Such remembering, however, can also be clouded by the discourse of nostalgia—and, as I have argued elsewhere,[2] by the discourses of purity and authenticity. It cannot incorporate present realities and hybridities into its logic, including the cultural hybridity and cosmopolitanism of many of its own citizens (such as Stephen Dedalus, Buck Mulligan, or Oscar Wilde)—for it would freeze Irishness in the nostalgic purity of a dead past, doomed to extinction in the face of modernity and history. How then can such a discourse deal with emigration—so important, after all, in Irish cultural history—unless it demand that (in Bruce Robbins's words) the eyes of the emigrant "can only be trained on his lost home" (Robbins 95)? For it is the native "soil" and the homeland (so consecrated in Irish songs as "the holy sod," "the holy ground," "the wee bit of green," and so on) that have to remain the only touchstones possible, the only images that can be allowed to be in one's memory continually, in order to maintain a nostalgic cultural identity that denies the existence of any other sorts of experience as genuine and acceptable.

This logic present a real dilemma for any Irish subject who, like Gabriel Conroy (in "The Dead") or like Joyce himself, interacts with modern English or continental cultures, but especially so for the Irish exile—whether wild goose or emigrant—who is away from home but who wishes to maintain his or her "Irishness." "The wild goose, Kevin Egan of Paris" in *Ulysses* (*U* 3.164) is a case in point: a portrait of the Fenian Joseph Casey who was imprisoned for his involvement in acts of Fenian violence in England (see Gifford 52), Joyce's Kevin Egan is a Fenian espousing the discourse of Irish nationalism and authenticity, but ironically stranded in the center of internationalism and cosmopolitanism, Paris. This is an irony not lost on his son Patrice, Stephen's friend, who tells Stephen: "—*C'est tordant, vous savez. Moi, je suis socialiste. Je ne crois pas en l'existence de Dieu. Faut pas le dire a mon père*" (*U* 3.169–70; my translation: "It's hilarious, you know. Me, I'm a socialist. I don't believe in the existence of God. Don't tell my father that"). Like Patrice, Stephen too is a freethinker living in Paris, eating *mou en civet* in his "Latin quarter hat" "when I was in Paris, *boul'Mich*'" (*U* 3.174–79). The Boulevard Saint-Michel, a major boulevard in the Latin Quarter on the Seine's Left Bank, was of course "the cafe center of student and bohemian life at the turn of the century" (Gifford 53). In such an environment, the Fenian Kevin Egan tries to hold on to "home" and to the memory of the past: at Rodot's patisserie (9 Boulevard Saint-Michel; Gifford 54), he speaks to Stephen "Of Ireland, the Dalcassians, of hopes, conspiracies, of Arthur Griffith" (*U* 3.226–27). And he complains about the degeneracy and sexual excess of Parisians:

> Licentious men. The *froeken*, *bonne à tout faire*, who rubs male nakedness in the bath at *Upsala. Moi faire*, she said, *tous les messieurs*. Not this *monsieur*, I said. Most licentious custom. Bath a most private thing. I wouldn't let my brother, not even my own brother, most lascivious thing .... Lascivious people. (*U* 3.234–38)

The repeated refrain of "Lascivious people"—in the context of massages and baths—suggests a paranoid fear of the foreign and the degenerate ("the fleshpots of Egypt"), all embodied in the Parisian bohemianism and cosmopolitan freethinking indulged in by Stephen and indeed by Egan's own son Patrice. Rather, Egan tries to teach his son "to sing *The boys of Kilkenny*" (*U* 3.257) and to keep his mind focused on "home," as defined by a discourse identifying Irishness as the agrarian, Catholic, and republican west of Ireland, the nostalgic discourse glorified by the Fenianism through which he defines himself. As Stephen ruefully notes, "In gay paree he hides, Egan of Paris, unsought by any save by me .... They have forgotten Kevin Egan, not he them. Remembering thee, O Sion" (*U* 3.249–50, 263–64). Like the Israelites remembering Zion by the rivers of Babylon, Egan continues to train his eyes on the past and on the native soil of an authentic Ireland, trying not to forget, while he is stranded by the boulevards of a latter-day Babylon. Unable to admit or incorporate hybrid and foreign experiences as part of his own complex identity, he lives in an "authentic" past already frozen in nostalgia.

So what the subject race, and the recalcitrant subject (like Kevin Egan) of a resistant colony, really hold on to, what they "remember," Joyce shows us, is not actual memories, so much as rosy-tinted sentimentalism and nostalgia—which is itself a "forgetting" of sorts. This is also true of the so-called "Citizen" in the "Cyclops" episode and of the particular brand of nationalist discourse which he espouses and represents. Much has been written and argued about the "Cyclops" episode (including by myself), and I won't go into great detail here, except to recall that, in the episode, Joyce illustrates the ways in which the Citizen's prototypically macho qualities of physical strength and retributive violence get repeatedly senti-mentalized and idealized, through selective and distorted "remembering," into national legendry, the very stuff Joyce is parodying. Satirizing the xenophobic views of radical Celticists such as Michael Cusack (the real-life model for the Citizen), Joyce's parodies repeatedly take on the forms of the nineteenth-century Irish nationalist literature which had sentimental-ized stereotypes of a "national character" (as Seamus Deane points out), usually bathed in a nostalgia for origins—what Homi Bhabha calls "that attempt to hark back to a 'true' national past" (Bhabha 303)—through what David Lloyd calls "the recurrent reproduction of Celtic material as a thematica of identity" (Lloyd 85). This harking back to a nostalgia for national origins rewrites Irish history into one, long, seamless tradition in which the endpoint is, of course, "A Nation Once Again" (even though there never was, historically, an Irish nation previous to 1922: see Cheng, *Joyce* 215–217). In "Cyclops," we find a number of extended and hilarious send-ups of such sentimentalized, nostalgia-laden, heroic Irish literature and legendry in the Celtic-revival mode, taking off everyone from James Clarence Mangan to Douglas Hyde. For example, one of the best-known of these parodies—obviously suggesting that the Irish are the greatest race on earth and are responsible for all the world's great achievements— lists in its catalogue of "the tribal images of many Irish heroes and hero-ines of antiquity" (*U* 12.175 ff.) such "Celtic" greats as Dante Alighieri, Christopher Columbus, Saint Brendan, Muhammad, "Brian Confucius," "Patrick W. Shakespeare," and so on.[3]

Similarly, Benedict Anderson has made the point that nations tend to construct themselves as "imagined communities" with a cohesive national character, sovereignties retrospectively endowed with a revisionist history of antiquity and racial purity: "[They] always loom out of an immemorial past, and, still more important, glide into a limitless future. It is the magic of nationalism to turn chance into destiny" (Anderson 11–12). As Anderson points out in his resonant discussion of Renan's use of "memory" and "forgetting," the favorite metaphor of emerging nations newly "re-discovering" their supposedly "forgotten," ancient pasts (consider the Celtic "Revival") is "sleep" (or "remembering"/reviving what had been forgotten): "[No other metaphor] seemed better than 'sleep,' for it permitted those intelligentsias and bourgeoisies who were becoming conscious of themselves as Czechs, Hungarians, or Finns [or, we might add, Celts] to figure their study of Czech, Magyar, or Finnish [or Celtic] languages, folklores, and musics as 'rediscovering' something deep-down always known" (196). But in order to *rediscover* something, you must have first *forgotten* it. In this discursive process, the newly "reawakened" national discourse "remembers" what it had forgotten by constructing a nostalgic revisionism which, like Renan's national forgetting of brutal past massacres, glosses over the brutalities of the past as well as the existence of minority groups not fitting the imagined national identity—by imagining for the island a historically continuous community with a homogenous national character. Thus, Irish national

> history rewrites itself as one long "Irish" tradition (with mists of inevitability)—in which the differences between Milesians, Gaels, Celts, and even Danes and Spaniards get written out; in which the Anglo-Irish get bracketed; in which Jews get written out altogether (in spite of their material presence in one's midst); and in which the purity of an Irish "race" is proclaimed in spite of the fact that there never was such a thing as an Irish "nation" and in spite of the many racial/ethnic interminglings of the extended, pluralistic contact zone known as "Ireland". (Cheng, *Joyce* 216–17)

As I have argued elsewhere, this sort of nativist nationalism is a nostalgic "remembering" which Joyce decries as "the old pap of racial hatred": "What race, or what language," Joyce wrote, "can boast of being pure today? And no race has less right to utter such a boast than the race now living in Ireland" (*CW* 165–66).

* * *

Let me now return for a moment to the topic of amnesia. As with my own "amnesia fantasies" as a youth, Stephen Dedalus would like to slough off the nightmare of history which so weighs him down and from which he cannot awake. But, like Luria's mnemonist, he remembers too much, is much too keenly aware of the pawnshop of history that is Ireland. Indeed, Joyce shows us how the losers—the victims of colonialism—need desperately to remember, to hold on to the past, cannot afford to forget; but he also shows how such "remembering" is itself a distortion and travesty of historical memory. Rather, at the level of nations and empires, the fascination with amnesia is a collective will to forget the unpleasantnesses of the past on the part of the *winners*, a Renanesque drive for national or imperial unity by forgetting the atrocities of the past. For Renan, this was a necessity for communal and national harmony. For Joyce, this is an elision of minority positions and groups that don't fit into the dominant view of national unity (as with Deasy's claim about the Jews not existing in Ireland).

I would like at this point to return to Nietzsche's and Yerushalmi's questions about how much we should remember and how much we should forget: "Given the need both to remember and to forget, where are the lines to be drawn? ... How much history do we require? What kind of history? What should we remember, what can we afford to forget, what must we forget? These questions are as unresolved today as they were then; they have only become more pressing" (Yerushalmi 107). Joyce's *Ulysses*, indeed, points out the dangers of *both* forgetting and remembering, for in *Ulysses* even "remembering," as we have seen, is a kind of forgetting, a Renanesque covering-up of brutal realities and facts. Both Renanesque versions of national "forgetting"/unity (as with Deasy) and Irish nationalist "remembering"/nostalgia (as with Kevin Egan and the Citizen) gloss over the complex realities of the diverse composition and frequently "corpsestrewn" material realities of the Irish people and their history.

IMAGINING/REMEMBERING THE NATION? "OR ALSO LIVING IN DIFFERENT PLACES"

In the rest of this chapter, I would like to pursue the complex realities of national "memory" and imagination by considering what Joyce's works, especially *Ulysses*, can tell us about the nation-state—by exploring the place of, well, *place*—or "places" (in the sense of different spaces and places)—in retroactively imagining and defining the Irish "nation." In the process, I will discuss how "place" and space have—in Irish historical "memory"—shaped and modulated the processes of imagining the nation through a series of binary oppositions, including the relationships in the

Irish national imaginary between: rural space versus urban space; outside versus inside—and outsiders versus insiders; emigrants (going outside) versus immigrants (coming inside); North versus South; and finally, past versus future (as discursive spaces in the national imaginary).

* * *

When Leopold Bloom walks into the newspaper office in the "Aeolus" episode of *Ulysses* and wonders aloud what all the other men are laughing about, Professor MacHugh names Dan Dawson's nationalist speech, "Our Lovely Land" as the source of their amusement. "—Whose land? Mr Bloom said simply. /—Most pertinent question, the professor said" (*U* 7.271–73). It is a most pertinent question indeed. Bloom—a Jew in Catholic Ireland—is repeatedly treated (and mistreated) by his fellow Irishmen as an undesirable alien, as someone from some *other* place, even though he is an Irish citizen born in Ireland. In our own contemporary world of refugee camps, displaced migrants, boat people, political prisoners and the USA Patriot Act, who belongs—indeed, who has rights—in the nation-state continues to be a most pertinent question and a central human rights concern: the role of the Outsider—the stranger from somewhere else, some other place—within the national imaginary, within the imagined authenticity, the imagined ethnic/racial/national identity, of the nation-state, so often used as an exclusionary tool against "outsiders." Think, after all, how much this issue is at the core of many international debates and controversies in recent years—such as the treatment of unwanted populations, foreign immigrants, and guest workers (from the Irish "Travelers" to Turkish guest workers in Switzerland to the thousands of migrants and refugees fleeing the war in Syria)—or such as the ethnic intolerance and ethnic genocides in countries such as Bosnia, Rwanda, Somalia, Iraq, Sudan, Nigeria, and the Central African Republic. At the core of all these debates and controversies is the militant belief in a narrowly definable and "authentic" ethnic or national identity that must exclude others from the tribe or the *polis* or the *patria*, an exclusionary national identity and xenophobia in whose name human rights can be violated and human blood can be shed in huge quantities, under the mantle of "nation" and under the pretext of "patriotism."

How citizenship and rights are defined (which is to say, how the "nation" is imagined and defined) has, of course, long been a central issue in Irish history. What does it mean to be Irish? Who qualifies as "Irish?"

What *is* Ireland? What is a nation? These are crucial questions which form a key subtext of *Ulysses*, especially in the "Aeolus" and "Cyclops" episodes, evoking the controversy then raging in turn-of-the-century Ireland regarding who could qualify as being "truly" Irish. This was an issue frequently discussed in Arthur Griffith's *United Irishman*, articulating the Celticist debate in the Nationalist revival—in which the racial purists argued that "only Gaels" were truly Irish, as opposed to the more liberal viewpoint that any "Irish-born man" should be considered Irish. As Don Gifford (130) points out: "It is interesting that the purist position would deny the distinction 'Irish' to many outstanding Irish-born people, including Swift, Sheridan, and Burke, Grattan and the members of his Parliament, Wolfe Tone and most of the United Irishmen, Parnell, Yeats and Synge, the Irish-born Italian Nannetti, and of course, the Irish-born Bloom." Joyce found such arguments for racial purity ridiculous; he had written his brother Stanislaus from Trieste that he would consider himself a Nationalist if it weren't for the Celticist insistence on the Irish language (Gaelic)—and if Griffith's newspaper weren't, in Joyce's words, "educating the people of Ireland on the old pap of racial hatred" (*Letters* II, 187).

But what defines Irishness? Is it Irish blood (a tautological concept in itself)? Is it residence in Ireland, in the actual space of the nation (but then how about all the wild geese and emigrants)? Is it the speaking of Gaelic? What are the essentials or essences needed to qualify as "Irish"? And who gets to say what qualifies as genuinely Irish? The issue of defining "Irishness" was a central one in Joyce's own time, witnessing the attempts by a nationalist movement to forge a national identity—and is still a visceral and urgent issue in Ireland today, with the continuing debates about the positions of North and South, Catholic and Protestant, republican and unionist, citizen and emigrant, the place of Irish Americans, and so on. Is perhaps the best we can do Leopold Bloom's vague and hapless vacillation that "A nation is the same people living in the same place .... Or also in different places" (*U* 12.1417–31)?

*   *   *

Let me begin by invoking Benedict Anderson's important and thought-provoking formulation of "nation" as an "imagined community": in the case of Joyce's Ireland, the Irishmen Bloom encounters repeatedly imagine an Irish nation as a cohesive community of Celtic racial origins and Irish national character—much like the holy triad of Catholic religion, nationalism, and the land espoused by the post-1922 agenda of "Irish Ireland"—in spite of the palpable, material reality and presence within their midst of non-conforming variants such as Leopold Bloom, Reuben J. Dodd, Joseph Nannetti, W. B. Yeats, and Charles Stewart Parnell. Although the entire community of a nation necessarily encompasses a great spectrum of heterogeneous characters and difference, yet too often nations imagine themselves as somehow inherently (and essentially), uniquely, "authentic" and different from each other, and therefore rivals and competitors. Joyce, as I have argued elsewhere, does at least posit the desirability of a more culturally inclusive alternative to the limits of a narrowly defined Irish nation.

The discrepancies and tensions between two particular kinds of cultural space—city life and country life—have long been crucial in the construction of Irishness and Irish national identity, of the "imagined community." The English imperial discourse had long fashioned the Irish as a primitive and uncivilized Celtic Other that served as a convenient foil for the supposedly "civil" and "civilized" English "citizen" (all terms derived from *civitas*, Latin for city). In response, the Gaelic Revival searched for many of the same elements (of rural primitivism) in "the true Celtic other within," thus mirroring the English stereotypes of the Celt. "The Gaelic *Ur*-ground," as anthropologist Lawrence J. Taylor calls it, thus "was to be sought on such outposts as the Arans, west of Galway, or the Blaskets, off the southwest Kerry coast"; it was in such rural outposts and spaces (and certainly not in Dublin or Cork [not to speak of Belfast]), that both anthropologists and the public came to look for "'authentic' voices .... of a pure western, primitive wisdom" (Taylor 216).

In the case of an "authentic" Irish national identity, what frequently resulted was a construction of Irish national identity and "national character" around the idealization of a rural and primitive West, a rural, Catholic, agrarian identity: "Like other forms of pastoral," Declan Kiberd notes, "this complex of ideas was a wholly urban creation, produced by such artists as W.B. Yeats and George Russell and by such political thinkers as Eamonn de Valera and Michael Collins. They were, to a man, the urbanized descendants of country people, and they helped to create the myth of a rural nation" ("Periphery" 5). And the emerging Irish Catholic middle class embraced this sentimentalized national mythology about rural Ireland as the authentic Ireland.

The critical problem with such a discursive logic is that the concept of a rural, Gaelic, peasant authenticity implies and mandates the existence of its opposite, the inauthentic, the fake, the non-authorized. In his seminal and influential 1892 lecture "The Necessity for De-Anglicising Ireland," Douglas Hyde had helped shape the subsequent discourse of the Gaelic Revival and the Gaelic League about the Irish nation in terms that were quite explicit, essentialist, exclusive: as Hyde wrote famously, "[W]e must strive to cultivate everything that is most racial, most smacking of the soil, most Gaelic, most Irish, because in spite of the little admixture of Saxon blood in the north-east corner, this island *is* and will *ever* remain Celtic at the core." (Note that Hyde's formulation clearly marks the space of Northern Ireland—"the north-east corner"—as an inauthentic deviation from true Irishness and the authentic national identity.) This rhetoric linking soil, nation, and race—as in the epigraph of *The Nation* newspaper, "racy of the soil"—is a quasi-religious discourse in which the rural countryside is transcended into a holy ground of originary and inherited sacredness. The rural space, especially the West, thus becomes the place, the site of the imagined nation. In such a discursive schema, there is no room for those others living, not on the authentic and racy soil, but on the consequently "inauthentic" and deracinated pavements and cobblestones of the un-Irish city. It is here that the violence of discourse (in Derrida's sense) takes place—and where Joyce, despite his considerable sympathies with the nationalist movement, parted company with a Gaelic nationalism weaned, as he put it, on "the old pap of racial hatred." For by valorizing some things as authentic or essential one necessarily brands other things—a feminine oral tradition, say, or Protestants, Italians, and Jews—as inessential, illegitimate, un-Irish. Kiberd has remarked that "the ludicrous category *un-Irish* was among [the] weird achievements" of the narrow-gauge nationalists (*Inventing* 337). Various forms of sport, literature, dance, and so on—as well as ethnic or racial heritages (Jewish, Italian, Anglo-Irish, black)—thus risked being denounced as "un-Irish." Yet what does it really mean to be an "inauthentic" Irish person, or an "un-Irish" Irish citizen? It *is* a positively bizarre category, that of the inauthentic Irishman. It is one thing to have urban guilt—as with Gabriel Conroy's *seoninism* in *The Dead*—over not being sufficiently in touch with the rural West. But it is another thing when the rhetoric of authenticity is used by ethnic nationalisms to discriminate against an Irish Jew born in Ireland, or—as we have seen too often in the twentieth century—used to justify acts of "ethnic cleansing" and other Human Rights violations.

*   *   *

Leopold Bloom is an example of such "inauthentic" Irishness within the nation-state, who must not even be allowed to claim to be "Irish." For Bloom is, in a sense, a hybrid, borderless, non-placed creature of cultural inauthenticity, lacking anything fixed and local about him: he is a freethinking Hungarian Jew who has been baptized both Catholic and Protestant, an urban dweller of foreign descent with intellectual pretensions—he is, in short, everything that Michael Cusack (head of the Gaelic Athletic Association and model for the "Citizen" in the "Cyclops" episode) or Daniel Corkery (as founder of the Irish Ireland movement) would repudiate as cosmopolitan, alien, and thus not native and Irish. In the "Cyclops" episode, our "citizen of the world" (Bloom) has a heated confrontation with the "Citizen" of a narrowly defined Irish nation. The latter accuses Bloom of "Swindling the peasants ... and the poor of Ireland. We want no more strangers in our house" (*U* 12.1150–51). Here the Citizen invokes the familiar binary behind xenophobia: strangers/foreigners, versus our house; outside versus inside; "them" versus "us." "Strangers in our house" was a term used of course to refer to the British, for Yeats's Cathleen had complained about "Too many strangers in the house .... My land was taken from me .... My four beautiful green fields" (the four provinces)—lines Stephen Dedalus had also referred to earlier ("Gaptoothed Kathleen, her four beautiful green fields, the stranger in her house" in *U* 9.36–37). Thus, the Citizen's narrow logic is unable to distinguish the English invaders from Bloom, an Irishman born in Ireland. Even more ironic is the reality that the Irish themselves are *all* foreigners—all from some other place—having been descended from Celts, Danes, Saxons, and so on, who each in their turn had once been "strangers in our house." The Citizen continues: "—The strangers .... Our own fault. We let them in. We brought them in. The adulteress and her paramour brought the Saxon robbers here .... A dishonoured wife, ... that's what's the cause of all our misfortunes" (*U* 12.1156–65). This is exactly the same logic as that of the Ulsterman Deasy's attack on women earlier (U 2.389–97), in its combination of racism, xenophobia, and misogyny—for all three of these are binary, totalizing structures which mirror each other, whether espoused by Celticist nationalist (the Citizen) or pro-English Ulsterman (Deasy). All of these binary structures get focused in the person of the Citizen and his ideology.

The Citizen needs to believe in a distinct and separable binary opposition between the pure and the hybrid, between friend and foe, between the self and the other, the Irish and the non-Irish: "—*Sinn Fein!* says the citizen. *Sinn fein amhain!* The friends we love are by our side and the foes we hate before us" (U 12.523–24). In citing the slogan of the Fenian movement (*Sinn Fein amhain*, "ourselves alone"), the Citizen is also reflecting a narrow-gauge, exclusivist rejection of Irish hybridity and polyculturalism, its fear and distrust of difference, its relegation of even some Irish citizens born in Ireland (like Bloom, Yeats, and Synge) to being "strangers in our house" (*U* 12.1151). Rather, Bloom is seen as dissembling and inauthentic, a creature from some other place altogether: "—A wolf in sheep's clothing, says the citizen. That's what he is. Virag from Hungary! Ahasuerus I call him. Cursed by God" (*U* 12.1666–67). Here we have the anti-Semitic distrust of the Wandering Jew (Ahasuerus) so long associated with otherness and homelessness, that race of shiftless exiles cursed by God to roam the earth, never having a home or place to call one's own, thus barred from any legitimate claim to nation or citizenship.

Predictably, the Citizen's ideology is one that invokes both violence and machismo:

> —We'll put force against force .... We have our greater Ireland beyond the sea [America] .... the *Times* rubbed its hands and told the whitelivered Saxons there would soon be as few Irish in Ireland as redskins in America .... Ay, they drove out the peasants in hordes. Twenty thousand of them died in the coffinships. But those that came to the land of the free remember the land of bondage. And they will come again and with a vengeance, no cravens, the sons of Granuaaile, the champions of Kathleen ni Houlihan. (*U* 12.1365–75)

In invoking the racialized trope of the Irish as Israelites (remembering the land/house of bondage) and as "redskins," the Citizen is nevertheless and simultaneously slurring the actual Jew in his midst as a "coon" and racial Other. But Bloom responds with a reasoned argument that force engenders force, that violent persecution creates hatred among nations which results in new cycles of retributive violence and persecution:

> —Persecution, says he, all the history of the world is full of it. Perpetuating national hatred among nations.
> —But do you know what a nation means? says John Wyse.
> —Yes, says Bloom .... A nation is the same people living in the same place .... Or also in different places.
> —What is your nation if I may ask? says the citizen.
> —Ireland, says Bloom. I was born here. Ireland. (*U* 12.1417–31)

Here, Bloom is forced to try to answer the question Ernest Renan famously asked, *Qu'est-ce qu'une nation?* As we have seen, nations tend to retrospectively construct themselves as imagined communities with a national essence, character, and identity, resulting in a value-laden hierarchy that writes out or homogenizes non-conforming "others." Bloom, as one of those "others" which a narrowly Celticist nationalism would write out (even though, as he points out, he was born Irish), responds simply— in stark contrast to the Citizen's exclusivity about authentic Irish citizenship—that "A nation is the same people living in the same place"—or, in some cases, "in different places." While his flustered and bumbling answer is one the men make fun of, it is nonetheless significant and powerful in its tolerant breadth: by defining a nation simply as a people generally (but not always) within a particular geographical location, Bloom's answer refuses either to hierarchize or to "imagine" an essentialized community, but rather allows for personal or ethnic difference and heterogeneity without denying the status of "citizens" or "nationals" to anyone within (or sometimes without) the community. As David Cairns and Shaun Richards write about Bloom: "[He] is the living antidote to all denials and exclusions .... and, as Jew, presents a cosmopolitan alternative to an Ireland whose sense of self was increasingly locked into the conservatism of the Gaelic homeland" (135).

However mockable and hapless a vacillation Bloom's definition of "nation" may be, it is a position which seems to me considerably less hapless and rather more viable today, after the 22 May 1998 referendum—the "Good Friday Agreement" on Northern Ireland, with its broad, flexible takes on place, dwelling, and citizenship: for, in the key clause that finally cut the Gordian knot of the decades-long sectarian troubles, the Good Friday Agreement recognizes, among other things, "the birthright of all the people of Northern Ireland to identify themselves and be accepted as Irish or British, or both, as they may so choose."[4] In other words, you can be a citizen of the Republic of Ireland while living in a different place, the North—as well as simultaneously a citizen of the United Kingdom! It is a mind-blowing concept that unmoors citizenship and nationality altogether from any notion of place, space, and residence.

Since Michael Cusack was the founder of the Gaelic Athletic Association and "the man ... that made the Gaelic sports revival" (*U* 12.880), it is appropriate that one of the arguments the Citizen and Bloom engage in is over Irish and English sports: "So off they started about irish sports and shoneen games the like of lawn tennis and about hurley and putting the stone and racy of the soil and building up a nation once again all to that" (*U* 12.889–91). By 1904 the Gaelic Revival had extended the issue of Irish identity and the cause of "building up a nation once again" even into the realm of sports, "by labeling particular games as 'racy of the soil' and 'Irish,' and by 'banning' particular others as un-Irish or shoneen or English" (Cheng, *Joyce* 206). At this point, the men in the pub join in singing "the immortal Thomas Osborne Davis's evergreen verses (happily too familiar to need recalling here) *A Nation Once Again*" (*U*12.916–17).

Indeed, both "racy of the soil" and "A Nation Once Again" are attributed to Davis, the nineteenth-century Irish poet and patriot who founded a nationalist newspaper aptly titled *The Nation*—whose motto was "racy of the soil"—and who composed the "evergreen" verses of "A Nation Once Again" (happily too familiar, indeed, to need recalling). But the Citizen's invocation of Davis's slogan and song is very ironic, for, as Cairns and Richards note:

> In the prospectus for *The Nation*, Davis addressed "a nationality which may embrace Protestant, Catholic, and Dissenter, —Milesian and Cromwellian,— the Irishman of a hundred generations and the stranger within our gates"; hence, the motto of *[T]he Nation*, to foster Irish Nationality and make it "racy of the soil," pointed to a nationality based on residence and willingness to acknowledge Irish rights and duties. (35)

Which is to say that Davis, as one of the founding fathers of the nationalist movement and the author of what has become the unofficial anthem of the IRA, espoused, ironically, a notion of "A Nation Once Again" that was very much a Bloomian sort of nation, rather than the kind of nation espoused by the Citizen. A further irony is that Davis, as a Protestant, would have been barred from Irish citizenship within the narrowly constructed definition of the Irish nation espoused by the likes of Cusack and Corkery. As Cairns and Richards note further: "Davis's writings continued to disseminate the ideas upon which he had hoped to construct a new nationalism, and in particular the concept of inter-sectarian co-operation for which he personally became an emblem" (41). Such a version of Irish nationalism would have looked very different from the one codified later by the nationalist movement, and a lot more like both Bloom's and that of the Good Friday Agreement.

Indeed—and in conclusion—Leopold Bloom's broad notion of nation— "a people living in the same place ... or also in different places"—prefigures the global and transnational condition of the twenty-first-century nation-state, in which mobility and travel and multiple residency do not necessarily disqualify one from citizenship nor from rights ("flexible citizenship," as sociologist Aihwa Ong calls it). Such a broad vision resists a narrow definition of Irish citizenship based on exclusionary ideals, a flexible and "polytropical" notion of "nation" and "citizenship" based on multiple possible visions and versions of nationalism and national identity and national pride, representing a variety of ethnic, religious, and linguistic heritages, all of them proud to be called Irish (or American or English or Bosnian or Ukrainian or whatever), while transcending the corrosive rhetoric of exclusionary authenticity. Think of how differently an Irish Ireland, or the longstanding debates over Northern Ireland, or for that matter the culture wars in the USA, would look like if informed by Bloom's polytropical definition of nation and national identity. In other words, what I am suggesting is that *Ulysses*—as I hope I have shown—argues for a loose and flexible notion of nation and national identity, one that allows for a multiplicity of national identifications and definitions of citizenship (much like the messy but constructive flexibility outlined in the Good Friday Agreement), rather than a single, narrowly defined nationalism and rigid sense of place. Indeed, the "nation" and the national imaginary can and should contain multitudes, and can house and encompass—as Irish citizens—rural folk and city dwellers, Catholics and Protestants, foreign-born and native-born, emigrants and immigrants, North and South, republican and unionist—within the polytropical spaces and places of the Irish nation.

NOTES

1. Renan is, however, a controversial figure in postcolonial studies—for, like many of his contemporaries, he defended colonialism as a laudable institution bringing civilization to the darker races, arguing that "The regeneration of the inferior or degenerate races, by the superior races, is part of the providential order of things for humanity": see, for example, Edward Said, *Reflections on Exile: And Other Literary and Cultural Essays* (Granta 2001), pp. 418–19; and Robert Young, *Colonial Desire: Hybridity in Theory, Culture and Race* (London: Routledge, 1995), p. 69.
2. Vincent J. Cheng, *Inauthentic: The Anxiety over Culture and Identity* (New Brunswick: Rutgers University Press), especially pp. 46–61. The following two pages are adapted from this material.
3. The previous paragraph was partly adapted from various passages in *Joyce, Race, and Empire*, pp. 198–200.
4. The full text can be found easily—for example, at www.peaceaccords.nd.edu/provision/citizenship-reform-northern-ireland-good-friday-agreement

Works Cited

Anderson, Benedict. *Imagined Communities: Reflections on the Origin and Spread of Nationalism*. Revised edition. London: Verso, 1991.

Bhabha, Homi K. "DissemiNation: Time, Narrative, and the Margins of the Modern Nation." In *Nation and Narration*, ed. Homi K. Bhabha. London: Routledge, 1990. 291–322.

Cairns, David, and Shaun Richards. *Writing Ireland: Colonialism, Nationalism, and Culture*. Manchester: Manchester University Press, 1988.

Cheng, Vincent J. *Joyce, Race, and Empire*. Cambridge: Cambridge University Press, 1995.

———. *Inauthentic: The Anxiety over Culture and Identity*. New Brunswick, NJ: Rutgers University Press, 2004.

Deane, Seamus. "National Character and National Audience: Races, Crowds, and Readers." In *Critical Approaches to Anglo-Irish Literature*, eds. Michael Allen and Angela Wilcox. Totowa, NJ: Barnes & Noble, 1989. 40–52.

Ellmann, Richard. *James Joyce*. Revised edition. Oxford: Oxford University Press, 1982.

Gifford, Don, and Robert J. Seidman. *"Ulysses" Annotated: Notes for James Joyce's "Ulysses."* Revised edition. Berkeley: University of California Press, 1988.

Hyde, Douglas. "The Necessity for De-Anglicising Ireland." 1892. *Language, Lore and Lyrics, Essays and Lectures*. By Hyde. Ed. Breandan O Conaire. Dublin: Irish Academic Press, 1986.

Joyce, James. *A Portrait of the Artist as a Young Man: Text, Criticism, and Notes*, ed. Chester G. Anderson. New York: Viking, 1968.

———. *Ulysses*. Eds. Hans Walter Gabler et al. New York: Vintage, 1986.

———. *Stephen Hero*. Eds. John J. Slocum and Herbert Cahoon. New York: New Directions, 1959a.

———. *The Critical Writings of James Joyce*. Eds. Ellsworth Mason and Richard Ellmann. New York: Viking, 1959b.

———. *Letters of James Joyce*, II and III. Ed. Richard Ellmann. New York: Viking, 1966.

Kiberd, Declan. *Inventing Ireland: The Literature of the Modern Nation*. Cambridge, MA: Harvard University Press, 1995.

———. "The Periphery and the Center." In Waters 5–22.

Lloyd, David. "Writing in the Shit: Beckett, Nationalism, and the Colonial Subject." *Modern Fiction Studies* 35.1 (Spring 1989): 71–86.

Lukacher, Ned. *Primal Scenes: Literature, Philosophy, Psychoanalysis*. Ithaca, NY: Cornell University Press, 1986.

Luria, A. R. *The Mind of a Mnemonist: A Little Book about a Vast Memory*. New York: Basic Books, 1968.

———. *The Man with a Shattered World: The History of a Brain Wound*. Cambridge, MA: Harvard University Press, 1972.

Nietzsche, Friedrich. *From* "On the Uses and Disadvantages of History for Life." In Rossington and Whitehead 102–108.

Norris, Margot. "Narration Under a Blindfold: Reading Joyce's 'Clay'." *PMLA* 102.2 (March 1987): 206–215.

Renan, Ernest. "What Is a Nation?" Trans. Martin Thom. In Homi K. Bhabha, ed., *Nation and Narration*. 8–22.

Rickard, John S. *Joyce's Book of Memory: The Mnemotechnic of Ulysses*. Durham, NC: Duke University Press, 1999.

Robbins, Bruce. *Feeling Global: Internationalism in Distress*. New York: New York University Press, 1999.

Rossington, Michael and Anne Whitehead, editors. *Theories of Memory: A Reader*. Baltimore: Johns Hopkins University Press, 2007.

Said, Edward. *Reflections on Exile: And Other Literary and Cultural Essays*. London: Granta, 2001.

Taylor, Lawrence J. "'There Are Two Things That People Don't Like to Hear about Themselves': The Anthropology of Ireland and the Irish View of Anthropology." In Waters 213–226.

Waters, John Paul, ed, *Ireland and Irish Cultural Studies*. Special issue of *South Atlantic Quarterly* 95.1 (1996).

Whitehead, Anne. *Memory*. New York: Routledge, 2009.

Yerushalmi, Yosef Hayim. *Zakhor: Jewish History and Jewish Memory*. New York: Schocken Books, 1989.

Young, Robert. *Colonial Desire: Hybridity in Theory, Culture and Race*. London: Routledge, 1995.

CHAPTER 4

The Memory of the Past: National Memory and Commemoration

THE MEMORY OF THE BOYNE: KING BILLY, NATIONAL MEMORY, AND JOYCE

There is perhaps no single moment in Irish history more permanently etched into Irish folk memory—in both North and South—than the Battle of the Boyne, as meaningful today to Ulster Protestants as it was when it took place in 1690. In late 1689 the Williamite army, led by Marshal Schomberg, had secured the province of Ulster, while the Jacobite army, led by the deposed James II, was ensconced in Dublin. The Jacobite army was a mix of French troops and poorly trained Irish Catholics; the Williamites were reinforced by Danish mercenaries and by English, Scottish, and Dutch regiments. The real stakes in the war were really not so much about control of Ireland as about the larger, ongoing European power struggle between the Dutch and the English (among others) on one side, and Louis XIV's France on the other.

The Dutch Prince Willem, Prince of Orange and Count of Nassau—and now King William III of England—was frustrated by the slow progress of the war and decided to take personal charge of the Irish campaign. On June 14, 1690, William landed at Carrickfergus with 36,000 troops; he was welcomed enthusiastically by the local populations, who lit up the hills of Antrim and Down with bonfires to announce the news of the king's arrival. Soon his army began its march toward Dublin, as the Jacobites withdrew to the south bank of the River Boyne.

© The Author(s) 2018
V. J. Cheng, *Amnesia and the Nation*, New Directions in Irish and Irish American Literature, https://doi.org/10.1007/978-3-319-71818-7_4

The battle was fought on the first of July 1690 at the banks of the Boyne about four miles west of Drogheda. As the Williamite army tried to cross the river, they had to withstand three charges by James's cavalry in heavy—and often confused—fighting. William himself, having been slightly wounded in the right arm the previous day, drew his sword with his left and famously addressed the Inniskilling Cavalry (of Ulster Protestants) with the exhortation, "Men of Enniskillen, what will you do for me?" Indeed, William's bravery seems to have been a decisive factor, as he was wounded in the leg but refused to leave the field. James, by contrast, seeing that the day was beginning to go against his side, turned and retreated to Dublin—with his army soon following him in confusion and disarray.

The Battle of the Boyne has been, of course, repeatedly commemorated, in both the North and the South of Ireland, throughout most of Irish history—and is still remembered and celebrated each July in Northern Ireland during marching season, culminating with the Orange parade on July 12, as thousands of Orangemen march with blaring whistles and booming drums to honor the "glorious and immortal memory" of William III, while street murals throughout the North portray a heroic King Billy crossing the Boyne on his beautiful white horse. The iconic image behind all these murals and banners is the well-known 1778 painting by Benjamin West (see Fig. 4.1), depicting William on his white horse exhorting the troops, while Marshal Schomberg—on the bottom right of the painting—is dying from a fatal wound.

As a battle, however, the Battle of the Boyne was (as one contemporary website puts it) "not decisive in any way: it wasn't even about Ireland—yet it became one of the most iconic events in Irish history" (www.goireland. about.com); the *Oxford Illustrated History of Ireland* (edited by R.F. Foster) notes that the battle "was not an engagement of any great military significance, but it became an encounter of prime symbolic importance" (Foster, *Oxford* 152). So why is it so significant in Irish memory—celebrated by Ulster Protestants and reviled by Irish republicans? One recent Irish studies text suggests that "although not the most strategically important battle of the war, the Boyne entered folklore mainly because of the [contrasting] behaviour of the two kings"—with William fighting bravely alongside his army, with James fleeing before his troops were defeated and being thereafter known as the cowardly king (Goodby 35). Ian McBride, in "Memory and National Identity in Modern Ireland," has pointed out that in Ireland, "the interpretation of the past has always been

Fig. 4.1   "The Battle of the Boyne," painting by Benjamin West (1778)

at the heart of national conflict" and national identity; Ulster loyalism, he suggests, has been "constructed upon a grid of talismanic dates—1641, 1690, 1912—all underlining the durability of ethnic antagonism in Ireland, the unchanging threat posed by Roman Catholicism" (1); and, he notes, "the most common historical image on Orange banners is still William III" (26) on his white horse.

What gets remembered historically, what gets forgotten, and why? Recall Yosef Yerushalmi's questions: "How much history do we require? What kind of history? What should we remember, what can we afford to forget, what must we forget?" (107). Recall also that the nineteenth-century French historian Ernest Renan has suggested in his important and influential 1882 lecture *"Qu'est-ce qu'une nation?"* ("What Is a Nation?") that central to the ability of a people to live together as a nation is the process of forgetting—for "[u]nity is always effected by means of brutality" and so the maintenance of that unity requires a shared willingness to forget the brutal past. The ability of a nation's people to feel things in common depends on the erasing of the historical memories of discord and violence against each other. By contrast, the continuation of the Troubles in Northern Ireland was incited and facilitated for decades by the annual Orange marches by Protestants through Catholic neighborhoods each July, constantly *reminding* Catholics (that is to say, refusing to allow them to forget) their status as colonial subjects, provoking them with loud drumbeats and with images and murals of the victorious King Billy on his white horse at the Boyne. It is only when both sides are willing to begin the process of forgetting past atrocities that a peace process becomes possible. As Renan puts it, "It is good for everyone to know how to forget" (6).

*   *   *

Joyce's writing is suffused with matters of national/historical memory and commemoration, anticipating—I would argue—our contemporary investigations and theories of national memory. The memory of King Billy and the commemorations of the Battle of the Boyne are invoked at various points in the Joyce corpus—but most notably near the end of "The Dead," when Gabriel Conroy tells a funny anecdote about "the late lamented Patrick Morkan, our grandfather" and his horse named Johnny: "One fine day the old gentleman thought he'd like to drive out with the quality to a military review in the park" (*D* 207)—presumably a display of English military power (as the old man, having made his fortune by owning and operating a starch mill, seems to have developed pretensions to being "quality"):

> —Out from the mansion of his forefathers, continued Gabriel, he drove with Johnny. And everything went on beautifully until Johnny came in sight of King Billy's statue: and whether he fell in love with the horse King Billy sits on or whether he thought he was back again in the mill, anyhow he began to walk around the statue.
> Gabriel paced in a circle round the hall in his goloshes amid the laughter of the others. (*D* 208)

This equestrian statue of King Billy on College Green, by the main entrance to Trinity College, had been for two centuries the center of Williamite celebrations and commemorations of the defeat of the Jacobites at the Boyne. Gabriel, clad in his continental galoshes and circling round and round the hall in imitation of Johnny circling King Billy's white horse, is thus unknowingly reinscribing the marks of an Irish cycle of paralysis, of satellitic subservience to (and cooption by) the Empire.

During the eighteenth century, state-sponsored Williamite celebrations and festivities occurred regularly throughout much of Ireland. In Dublin, "a vice-regal levee [was] held at the Castle, followed by a procession of notables to the equestrian statue of William III at College Green"; the First of July was "marked with bonfires, fireworks, the wearing of Orange cockades and ritual toasts to King William's memory ... [and] marches through the main thoroughfares of Dublin" (McBride 18). That equestrian statue of King Billy on College Green had a long and troubled history as a symbol of historical commemoration, despised by Catholics as a hated symbol of English domination and of the defeat at the Boyne. As Adaline Glasheen points out (citing Gilbert's *History of Dublin*, III. 40–56): "In Dublin (before the Free State) the Ulstermen's brazen calf was a lead equestrian statue of King Billy on College Green which, on Williamite holy days, was painted white (a white horse in a fanlight is still a sign of Protestant sympathies) and decorated with orange lilies ... and green and white ribbons 'symbolically placed beneath its uplifted foot'" (Glasheen 309)—a provocative, symbolic act designed to remind Catholics of (again, refusing to let them forget) the subservience of the green to the orange, in the physical embodiment of King Billy and his horse. After the Union (1800), Catholic resentment and opposition to such Williamite commemorations grew—and Catholics retorted by repeatedly vandalizing and defacing King Billy's statue—and then in April 1836 succeeded in blowing the figure of the King off the horse (McBride 29; Glasheen 309). (The statue was later restored, but destroyed again in 1929).

Such Williamite celebrations—such as the eighteenth-century Orange parades on July 1 in Belfast or the marches in Dublin to the equestrian statue of King Billy on College Green—were, of course, state-sponsored commemorations organized by the dominant power, displays and versions of official memory and history centered around monuments and statues celebrating the greatness of the imperial past, what Nietzsche called "monumental history." Post-colonial scholars have distinguished between such official versions of nationalism, which mirror the ideology of British imperialism, "and the subaltern nationalism of the Gaelic underclass, as manifested in nineteenth-century street ballads and agrarian insurgency" (McBride 34). As Joep Leerssen points out: "For the best part of history, the native tradition in Ireland had no control over the dedication and monumentalisation of public space [such as the statue of King Billy or Nelson's Pillar or the Wellington memorial in Phoenix Park]; indeed, precisely in that condition do we find the very definition of its subaltern and oppressed situation. Catholic Ireland had no castle or cathedral to display its regimental flags or the monuments to its heroes ....The struggle for dominance in the public sphere between unionist and nationalist, between Protestant Ascendancy and Catholic middle classes, is a struggle for the public manifestation and controlling of monumentalised commemoration" (Leerssen 211). Hence the contentious skirmishes around that statue of King Billy on College Green.

Without any state-sanctioned, official versions of public commemoration and memory, Leerssen notes, "Remembrancing for Catholic, anti-British Ireland had for a long time been an informal communitarian concern, often in oral face-to-face transmission by way of balladry and folktale"; such "community remembrancing" is "sub-elite and demotic, carried largely by local or small-scale communities rather than by the elites ..., perpetuated by oral or folkloristic face-to-face means rather than mediatised in print or monuments" (Leerssen 214–215). Luke Gibbons has pointed out that Joyce's *Ulysses* is laced through with street ballads relating to nationalist insurgencies (especially 1798), songs such as "The Memory of the Dead" and "The Croppy Boy"; as Gibbons argues, this is "a kind of popular memory which has less to do with plenitude and authenticity" than with "what Foucault describes as 'subjugated knowledge': 'naive knowledges, located low down on the hierarchy'" (Gibbons, "Where ...," 156–158).

I would argue that, in "The Dead," Joyce is quite aware of the separate realms of official commemoration and of subaltern, republican memory. As both Gibbons and I have previously noted, "The Lass of Aughrim" is one such ballad and example of subaltern memory. Joyce's choice of this variant title/version of an old folk song allies it with the West of Ireland, for the town of Aughrim is about 30 miles from Galway, the hometown of both Gretta and Nora Barnacle. While Gabriel Conroy's thoughts repeatedly circle around *official* memory—in the form of the Wellington memorial in Phoenix Park and King Billy's equestrian statue on College Green—Gretta's memory "looks instead to a half-remembered street ballad to come to terms with an unfathomable loss" (Gibbons, *Transformations* 145). The song Gretta is listening to is a stunningly appropriate choice on Joyce's part in terms of subaltern nationalist memory, for "The Lass of Aughrim" is a song about mastery, domination, and mistreatment (even rape) of a peasant woman by a patriarchal nobleman. Thus, Gretta—like the Lass—herself becomes here a figure for Ireland and for the Catholic West, cruelly dominated and mistreated by patriarchal and imperial masters.

Furthermore, to Joyce and to his Irish readers the town of Aughrim should hold an even more potent symbolic value—for it is closely associated with the Battle of the Boyne and with the subjugation of Ireland by the English. The twelfth of July, popularly known as "White Horse Day" (for King Billy on his white horse), is celebrated still by Ulster Protestants as the victory at the Boyne in 1690 over the Jacobites. But that date and that battle are also associated and frequently confused with another (and more historically significant) battle, the Battle of Aughrim. As the *Encyclopedia Britannica* notes, although the Battle of the Boyne is celebrated on July 12, that date "is actually the old style date [in the Julian calendar] of the more decisive Battle of Aughrim in the following year," 1691. As R. F. Foster writes in *Modern Ireland 1600–1972*:

> [I]t is uncertain whether [the Boyne] was the decisive battle of the war, though Protestants celebrate it still. Jacobites saw it as an indecisive engagement, Aughrim a year later being "the great disaster" … all hope went after Aughrim, where [the Irish forces] lost the day in a welter of heroics, confusion, and alleged treachery: "the most disastrous battle in Irish history." … The losses were enormous, in what was to be the last pitched battle in Irish history. (*Modern* 148, 150)

It was the Irish defeat at Aughrim a year after the Boyne that finally and fully sealed English domination of Ireland. Aughrim, then, like the hapless Lass in the song, becomes itself a poignant symbol of domination and colonization by imperial patriarchs—that murdered Irish past, the dead, the bodies of, as Yeats wrote in his verse play *Purgatory*, "long ago/Men that had fought at Aughrim and the Boyne."[1]

How is history remembered and/or forgotten? Why has the Battle of the Boyne been commemorated for centuries while Aughrim has been largely forgotten or repressed? After all, Irish casualties at the Boyne "had not exceeded 1,000 and their forces still held Athlone and Limerick" (Duffy 121); it was hardly a decisive battle. Rather, it was the English victory at Aughrim a year later that decisively sealed the fate of Ireland—as "nearly 7,000 Irish were killed, making it as momentous a day in the Catholic folk memory as Boyne was for Protestants" (Duffy 121). The battle became known, in the Irish language, as *Eachdhroim an air*— "Aughrim of the slaughter." But, after all, it is the winners who get to choose what gets officially commemorated—and what gets relegated to suppressed, unofficial, subaltern memory. Some have suggested that, for the English and for Ulster Protestants, it was preferable to celebrate the Boyne, where both English troops and their king fought courageously and where conversely Irish troops (and their king) were more easily depicted as cowardly—than to celebrate Aughrim, where the Irish were killed in great numbers but where they also clearly fought with great courage.[2] Thomas Moore's ballad (in the *Irish Melodies*) about the Battle of Aughrim, "The Lamentation of Aughrim," begins with the poignant line: "Forget not the field where they perished"[3]—but, alas, official (as well as popular) history have indeed largely forgotten. For example, a recent publication titled *Irish Studies: The Essential Glossary* discusses the Battle of the Boyne at length—while noting that it was "not the most strategically important battle of the war" (Goodby 35)—but does not contain a single mention of Aughrim. And recently the Aughrim battlefield site became the subject of controversy over plans to build the new M6 motorway through the battle-field. While historians and environmentalists objected to the potential destruction of the battlesite, nevertheless the motorway was built and opened in 2009. But in "The Dead" Joyce inscribed the suppressed traces of unofficial, subaltern nationalist memory in the form of Gretta Conroy listening to an old song, "The Lass of Aughrim," a street ballad whose contents and title both conjure the suppressed memory of the dead, spe-cifically the courageous men who had fought and died at Aughrim in the West of Ireland.

Joyce's text is sensitive to the processes of national memory and national forgetting, in which Irish cultural memory has elevated the memory of a relatively inconsequential battle—the Boyne—to that of an iconic source of commemoration and memorialization, all the while that the most sig-nificant and decisive battle of the Williamite wars—Aughrim—has been largely forgotten.[4]

*   *   *

As we have seen in "The Dead," Joyce was very aware of King Billy and his white horse as symbols of official, English imperial power. I have writ-ten elsewhere (in *Joyce, Race, and Empire*[5]) about "horses" in Joyce's works, especially about the way "dark horses" (such as Throwaway and Leopold Bloom) are contrasted with the "white horse" of empire. Such an emblem of empire is especially appropriate if we remember that the "white horse" was the specific emblem of the House of Hanover, the English ruling dynasty (later the Windsors). Furthermore, the white horse was a personal symbol of William III, King Billy, the Protestant Prince of Orange, winner of the Battle of the Boyne and the scourge of Irish Catholics. In *Ulysses*, the particular symbolism of the uplifted foot of King Billy's white horse, ready to crush rebellious Irish Catholics, appears in "Wandering Rocks" when the vice-regal parade rounds College Green: "Where the foreleg of King Billy's horse pawed the air Mrs Breen plucked her hastening husband back from under the hoofs of the outriders" (*U* 10.1231–33). The effectively ambiguous syntax here suggests an equal danger to Dubliners of being crushed by King Billy's horse and by the vice-regal hooves—for they are both metonymies for the same thing, Imperial (and Protestant) England.

In "The Dead" Gabriel's thoughts—unlike Gretta's, which are focused on "The Lass of Aughrim" and on Michael Furey—repeatedly circle around two commemorative emblems of empire, two notable instances in Dublin of "monumental history": the Wellington memorial in Phoenix Park and King Billy's equestrian statue by Trinity College. These two figures—commemorating two English icons and conquerors, William III and the Iron Duke of Wellington—merge in *Finnegans Wake*: "This is the Willingdone on his same white harse, the Cokenhape ... his big wide harse" (*FW* 8.17, 21). Wellington and his big white horse are, as I have argued, the *Wake*'s prime symbols for the authority of empire; however, the "Willingdone" on his "big wide harse" is, as Adaline Glasheen has argued, "scarcely to be distinguished" from a number of imperial figures, including King Billy, William the Conqueror, and Kaiser Wilhelm. On *FW* page 135 HCE is described as a king: "Dutchlord, Dutchlord, overawes us ... like the prince of Orange and Nassau" with his "great wide cloak ... and his little white horse" (*FW* 135.08–22). The "Dutchlord" is both William III, King Billy on his white horse, the Dutch Prince of Orange and Count of Nassau who overawed Catholic Ireland at the Boyne—and another empire-mongering King William, Kaiser Wilhelm (*Deutschland, Deutschland über alles*). In another passage about battles and empire-building, we learn that "Hittit was of another time, a white horsday" (*FW* 347.02); McHugh glosses "White Horse Day" as "12 July in Ulster: King Billy on a White Horse," celebrated by Ulster Protestants as the victory at the Boyne over the papists. That equestrian statue of King Billy's white horse returns in the description of HCE as "a kingbilly whitehorsed in a finglas mill" (*FW* 75.15; McHugh notes that William III stayed at Finglas after the Battle of the Boyne).

"This is the Willingdone on his same white harse": in the celebrated "Museyroom" passage of *Finnegans Wake* (pages 8–10), the wax museum that is the "Willingdone Museyroom" (8.10) is dominated by Arthur, Duke of Wellington, on his big white horse, Copenhagen. The Iron Duke seated on his big white horse is, like all such equestrian statues, a stylized symbol of the power of authority. Around and below him are the Lipoleum(s), the three young insurgents who sometimes seem one. Thus, the Duke of Wellington is presented as an archetypal patriarch and wielder of authority and power, sitting on his high horse over the rebellious children who try to unhorse the Father and the Law of the Father, and make Humpty have a great fall. He is indistinguishable from King Billy at the Boyne, for he is "the big Sraughter Willingdone [both William and Wellington], grand and magentic in his goldtin spurs and his ironed dux [Iron Duke] and his quarter brass woodyshoes and his magnate's gharters" (*FW* 8.17–19; his Inniskilling Cavalry is also here in "inimyskilling" in 8.23). After all, "brass money and wooden shoes" were part of the famed Orange toast to William III that Stephen recalls in the "Nestor" episode: "To the glorious, pious and immortal memory of the Great and Good King William III, who saved us from popery, slavery, arbitrary power, brass money and wooden shoes" (see *U* 2.273). And, sure enough, two lines later we find the lipoleums described as "the three lipoleum boyne grouching down in the living detch" (*FW* 8.21–22): three rebellious boys crouching down on the ground in a living ditch (in the sod, as opposed to the Orange King on his high horse) waiting for King Billy at the Boyne. One of the three rebellious boys appears to be Indian: he is "the hinndoo Shimar Shin between the dooley boy and the hinnessy" (*FW* 10.03–7): between the Irish Hennessey and Dooley boys is an "Injun" (8.29) boy, a "hinndoo." Furthermore, I would argue that "Willingdone" is also a direct reference to Viceroy Willingdon, the 1st Marquess of Willingdon, who was Viceroy and Governor-General of India from 1931 to 1936—after having served, during a tempestuous period of civil unrest, as Governor of Bombay (1913–1918) and Governor of Madras (1919–1924). During the 1930s (as *Finnegans Wake* was being written) Willingdon, as Governor-General of India, forcibly suppressed the activities of Mahatma Gandhi and the Indian National Congress. Thus, Wellington on his white horse (as conqueror of India and defender of the empire) and King Billy (as conqueror of Catholic Ireland) and Viceroy Willingdon (as enforcer of British rule in India)—all unite, in Joyce's text, into a collective figure (in which Ireland and India are correspondingly united as a collective victim of English imperialism), a symbol of colonial domination and power politics. The centerpiece of the Museyroom is but a wax version of at least three famous equestrian statues that all symbolized imperial English rule: the statue of King Billy on College Green in Dublin; the giant Wyatt equestrian memorial to Wellington in London; and a large, bronze, equestrian statue (supposedly admired by Wellington) of Thomas Munro, Governor of Madras (1820–1827), in the center of Madras, India ("madrashattaras" in 10.16).

The Museyroom episode climaxes with the lipoleum's collective response to the "insoult on the hinndoo seeboy" (*FW* 10.14) by Willingdone and his horse. At this point, the "dooforhim seeboy" (the two-for-one trio, Irish and Indian—Hinnessy, Dooley, and the Hindu sepoy) picks up his "bombshoob" (*FW* 10.09) and uses it to close the episode: "This is the dooforhim seeboy blow the whole of the half of the hat of lipoleums off the top of the tail on the back of his big wide harse …. How Copenhagen ended" (*FW* 10.19–22). Like the Sepoy Mutineers in 1857, the incensed "seeboy" ("madrashattaras") rebels and blows the big white horse, emblem of imperial authority, to bits—by unhorsing the king and destroying his horse ("How Copenhagen ended").

Thus, in *Finnegans Wake* Indian colonial domination by, and resistance to, English imperial rule is re-presented (or co-presented) by Joyce as parallel to and synonymous with Catholic Ireland's relationship to Protestant England—for the "hinndoo" sepoy blowing up Willingdone's big white horse is but another version of Irish Catholic Hennesseys and Dooleys tarring, defacing, and then (in 1836) blowing up King Billy's white horse on Dublin's College Green. Joyce's texts suggest his understanding that the *lieu de memoire*—the site of historical commemoration—is a significant cultural battleground over who gets to control the memory of the dead, a space of historical conflict between official, monumental history and subaltern, insurgent memories. The Museyroom thus becomes a collective case study of colonial politics and the dynamics of power—in which the white horse is itself the symbolic site for this battle of politics, ideology, and power. Joyce—in "The Dead" and in *Finnegans Wake*—gives voice to suppressed, subaltern history and memory, in this struggle over insurgent, national memory and "monumental history"—focusing on the commemorative valences of equestrian statues like the one of King Billy and his horse.[6]

*   *   *

THE MEMORY OF 1916: HURLEYSTICKS, MARTYROLOGY, AND THE EASTER RISING

www.ireland.ie—the official website for the Easter Rising Centenary in Ireland—stated on its homepage in 2016:

> Each year at Easter, we remember and honour those who took part and gave their lives during the Easter Rising, and with the launch of an extensive programme of events, 2016 brings about a massive commemoration centred in the city where it all took place, Dublin.

The commemoration program was indeed "massive," beginning with the "synchronised wreath-laying ceremonies at strategic points around Dublin, starting with Dublin Castle." *The Irish Times* made a valiant attempt to help the interested individual, whether Irish citizen or visitor, sort through all the "official ceremonies and hundreds of local initiatives"—by listing, on its website, a selected and annotated list of "50 events for 2016." Such celebrations were widespread and worldwide: even the Hibernian Society in Salt Lake City, Utah (where I live), with the official imprimatur and financial backing of the Irish Consulate in San Francisco, programmed no less than ten events (including poetry readings, films, concerts, parades and so on) during spring 2016 in commemoration of the Rising. In Ireland, poems (by poets such as Paul Muldoon and Eavan Boland), plays, performances, songs, films, documentaries, television programs, and so forth were all officially commissioned for the 1916 ballyhoo. Which is to say that the massive and coordinated weight of official, governmental publicity—and memory-making—were all thrown behind the effort to commemorate and memorialize the Easter 1916 Rising. (This has not always been true.) So it is in some ways quite remarkable, and rather startling, that a brief and aborted uprising—questionably planned, clumsily botched, and quite unpopular with the general populace at the time (indeed, when the captured rebels were led through the streets of a bombed-out Dublin, they were spat on by the Dubliners)—that it could have, 100 years later, reached this high canonical, iconic status of state-sponsored commemoration and historical memorialization.

*   *   *

James Joyce had almost nothing to say about 1916 directly. Richard Ellmann reports that "Joyce followed the events with pity; although he evaluated the rising as useless, he felt also out of things"; his ambivalence was "balanced between bitterness and nostalgia," and he declined an invitation from a Swiss publication to write an analysis of the Rising (Ellmann II, 399). But 1916 has long been significant in Irish history for a number of other reasons, too, most notably (especially in the North) for the Battle of the Somme and the thousands of Irish soldiers who died in France at that battle. For Joyceans, 1916 also marks the publication of *A Portrait of the Artist as a Young Man*.

Neither *Portrait*, nor its earlier first-draft manuscript *Stephen Hero*, have really been discussed in terms of the later events in 1916.[7] But I would like to suggest that Joyce's *bildungsroman*, if not prophetic, at least anticipates the Easter Rising in a number of interesting ways. For the young Stephen Dedalus of *Stephen Hero* and *A Portrait*, any force that would constrict his personal freedom and development is suspect, including the Nationalist/Celticist movement. Stephen experiences the call of Celticism, a "voice [which] had bidden him to be true to his country and help to raise up her fallen language and tradition" (*P* 84)—but "The programme of the patriots filled him with very reasonable doubts; its articles could obtain no intellectual assent from him. He knew, moreover, that concordance with it would mean for him a submission of everything else in its interest" (*SH* 76–77).

In the nationalistic Daniels household and at University College, this Celticist voice hails Stephen and makes its appeal, in simultaneity with the priestly pressure hailing him with a religious calling; both voices pitch interpellated "vocations" which he distrusts. ("He himself was the greatest sceptic concerning the perfervid enthusiasms of the patriots" [*SH* 204].) The depiction of Mr. Hughes, the teacher of the Irish language class, is Joyce's portrait of the ardent, militant Celticist (*SH* 59–60):

> He spoke in a high-pitched voice with a cutting Northern accent. He never lost an opportunity of sneering at seoninism ["West Britonism," derived from Seon/John, esp. John Bull] and at those who would not learn their native tongue. He said that Beurla [English] was the language of commerce and Irish the speech of the soul .... He scoffed very much at Trinity College and the Irish Parliamentary party. He could not regard as patriots men who had taken oaths of allegiance to the Queen of England and he could not regard as a national university an institution which did not express the religious convictions of the majority of the Irish people.

Hughes was, of course, directly modeled on an actual Celtic-language teacher Joyce himself took lessons from for a short time: Padraic Pearse, the schoolmaster, language teacher, and poet who would, a few years later, become the primary leader and martyr of the Easter Rising.

To Stephen, the Celticist emphasis on Irish language and culture is a misdirected nostalgia for a glorious and idealized Celtic past and purity, within a binary logic and structure imposed by the English oppressors: a pure Celtic glory and Firbolg/Milesian origin to mirror and compete with the vaunted Anglo-Saxon racial purity erected by the other side. The Celticist logic is a binarity that seeks to deny/demean anything English and glorify everything Irish—as in Hughes's essentializing characterizations of English/Beurla as "the language of commerce and Irish [as] the speech of the soul."

The result of such binary logic is a romantic sentimentalization of all things Celtic, regardless of actual social realities and conditions. In *Portrait*, Stephen recalls the hostile Nationalistic audience's boos and catcalls during the infamous debut of Yeats's *The Countess Cathleen* at the Abbey Theatre: "A libel on Ireland!" "Made in Germany!" "Blasphemy!" "We never sold our faith!" "No Irish woman ever did it!" "We want no amateur atheists." "We want no budding buddhists" (*P* 226). Joyce, who *was* an amateur atheist and Buddhist sympathizer,[8] was himself in the audience and, unlike the hissers and booers, "clapped vigorously" (Ellmann I, 68–69)—refusing to see the world only through the shamrock-tinted glasses which would deny any possibility of Irish immorality or even imperfection.[9]

Stephen's young Nationalist friend Davin (called Madden in *Stephen Hero*)—based on Joyce's real-life friend George Clancy—is, however, trapped inside the powerful, binary logic of Celticism. Davin/Madden is the character in Joyce's works who perhaps most closely embodies the Celtic Revival's (and later Irish Ireland's) notion of the "authentic" Irish Celt—Davin, the peasant *ingenu* with "the rude Firbolg mind", "the young peasant [who] worshipped the sorrowful legend of Ireland" and whose "nurse had taught him Irish and shaped his rude imagination by the broken lights of Irish myth ... [with] the attitude of a dullwitted loyal serf"; as a result, "Whatsoever of thought or of feeling came to him from England or by way of English culture his mind stood armed against in obedience to a password: and of the world that lay beyond England he knew only the foreign legion of France in which he spoke of serving" (*P* 181). In effect, such a closed system is trapped within the oscillation of an English/Irish dialectic, in which everything is still defined around Englishness.

Stephen at one point thinks of Davin affectionately as a "rude Firbolg mind" with a "delight in rude bodily skill—for Davin had sat at the feet of Michael Cusack, the Gael" (*P* 180). Davin is an athlete and a sports enthusiast, disciple of Michael Cusack, the real-life founder of the Gaelic Athletic Association (and model for the xenophobic Citizen in *Ulysses*), whose championing of Irish sport was a central force in the Celticist movement. At the Irish language classes in *Stephen Hero*, Cusack, "A very stout black-bearded citizen ... was a constant figure at these meetings" (*SH* 61), along with Madden/Davin, "who was the captain of a club of hurley-players" as well as Arthur Griffith, "the editor of the weekly journal of the irreconcilable party" (*The United Irishman*). Stephen, who is not an athlete, perceives some relation between the movement's emphasis on sport/play and its liberationist ethos: "The liberty they desired for themselves was mainly a liberty of costume and vocabulary .... here he saw people playing at being free" (*SH* 62)—as "bodies of young Gaels conflicted murderously in the Phoenix Park with whacking hurley-sticks" (*SH* 62). Stephen's sarcastic observation to Madden/Davin about such emulative play: "—I suppose these hurley matches and walking tours are preparations for the great event." As an older Stephen would again reflect later in *Ulysses*, listening to the bellicose sounds of the schoolboys' hockey game in the "Nestor" episode, there is a direct correlation between war/combat and the playing fields of Eton or Clongowes: "Jousts. Time shocked rebounds, shock by shock. Jousts, slush and uproar of battles, the frozen deathspew of the slain, a shout of spearspikes baited with men's bloodied guts" (*U* 2.316–8).

Hurley, or hurling, the Irish national sport, is a rough and brutal sport with similarities to football, rugby, hockey, and lacrosse; and is still associated with Irish nationalism and the Irish language. In *Portrait*, Stephen, after first quoting ironically from the Fenian drill book ("—Long pace, fianna! Right incline, fianna! Fianna, by numbers, salute, one, two!"), then comments to Davin/Madden about the relations between Fenian drills, revolutions, and hurley: "—When you make the next rebellion with hurleysticks ... and want the indispensable informer, tell me. I can find you a few in this college" (*P* 202). Indeed, the "next rebellion" and "the great event" would arrive just a few years later in the form of the Easter Rising—in which some of the Irish rebels were armed only with pikes, not much more effective than hurleysticks.

At the very end of *Portrait*, as Stephen is preparing to leave for Paris, he notes in a diary entry that he "Met Davin at the cigar shop .... He was in a black sweater and had a hurleystick. Asked me was it true I was going away and why. Told him the shortest way to Tara was *via* Holyhead" (*P* 250). Stephen's cryptic response to Davin's question suggests his conviction that the road to Irish freedom (the traditional Irish seat at Tara) was to be found not through the hurleystick of Irish Nationalism carried by Davin, but via Holyhead, the closest port outside Ireland on the way to the Continent. It is there that Stephen hopes to "discover the mode of life or of art whereby [his] spirit could express itself in unfettered freedom" (*P* 246)—so as "to forge in the smithy of my soul the uncreated conscience of my race" (*P* 253).

Easter 1916—a rising whose military operations were largely in the hands of three minor poets (Pearse, Joseph Plunkett, Thomas MacDonagh)—was exactly the sort of hurleystick match (or mismatch) that Stephen had predicted as the "great event" and the "next rebellion with hurleysticks." In *Portrait*, Davin observes that "They [Tone, Parnell, and other Irish patriots] died for their ideals, Stevie .... Our day will come yet, believe me" (*P* 203). The poignant irony of Davin's comment—in a retrospective coloring—must have given Joyce pause in later life: for their day would indeed come to die for their ideals. Among Joyce's patriot friends, both the character of MacCann, based on Joyce's friend, the popular pacifist/feminist/nationalist Francis Sheehy Skeffington, whom Joyce told Stanislaus was the cleverest man at University College (Ellmann II, 61)—and Davin, based on Joyce's friend George Clancy—would become Irish martyrs: Skeffington was shot to death by a British officer at Portobello Barracks during the Easter Rising; and Clancy, after becoming mayor of Limerick, would be murdered in his own house and in front of his family by the English Black and Tans (see *Portrait* 522–23). As Joyce had predicted, the hurleystick rebellions would prove no match for British military power, giving birth instead only to Yeats's "terrible beauty."

*   *   *

The quality of martyrdom in the "hurleystick rebellion" of 1916 was neither accidental nor unintended—for, if the character of Hughes in *Stephen Hero* was modeled after Padraic Pearse, Pearse himself had his own models: not only Cuchulain (as Yeats had noted in "The Statues") but also, most notably, Robert Emmet and Jesus Christ.

Robert Emmet, the hero of 1803: there are, of course, many similarities between the uprisings of 1798–1803 and 1916. Indeed, Pearse ("This man kept a school," as Yeats reminded us in "Easter 1916") had established

St. Enda's in the Hermitage, Rathfarnham, because of that estate's associations with Emmet (there, as Roy Foster has noted, "an obsession with Robert Emmet took over"; *Modern* 459); and many of Pearse's plans for Easter 1916 were modeled on Emmet's own uprising in the Irish capital. Both 1803 and 1916 involved a small body of poorly armed Irish patriots trying to resist the military power of the British Empire (many of the Irish rebels in 1803 had only pikes as weapons, as was also true of some of the 1916 rebels [Kee, *Ireland*, 161]); as military operations, both were poorly planned and badly, almost farcically, executed (indeed, disagreement among its leaders forced the 1916 Rising to be moved from Easter Sunday to the next day, with resulting confusion and consequently only half the expected number of volunteers showing up the next day)[10]; in both cases, the rebels failed to seize a very lightly guarded Dublin Castle (which would have been significant, both strategically and symbolically); an 1803 proclamation printed in the name of the "Provisional Government" would influence Pearse's 1916 Proclamation of Independence; and both rebellions depended hopefully—but in the end futilely—on foreign aid and reinforcements that never quite materialized (from the French in 1798 and 1803, from the Germans in 1916). And, in both cases, the martyred rebels became canonized as national heroes whose symbolic sacrifice would inspire nationalist revolution, resulting eventually in the creation of the Irish Free State.

In the "Sirens" episode of Joyce's *Ulysses*, Leopold Bloom notices "Robert Emmet's last words" in a shop window (and, as we know, farts while reading them). An episode later, in "Cyclops," we get an extended and parodic account of Robert Emmet's last moments.[11] Emmet, of course, was hanged and beheaded on September 20, 1803 (after a farcical and doomed attempt at capturing Dublin Castle), in what was a brutally botched public execution, after speaking his famous last words ("When my country takes her place among the nations of the earth then and not till then, let my epitaph be written. I have done")—and, as a result of this hopeless melodrama involving a minor historical figure, has since been somehow—incredibly—raised to the highest mythological pantheon of legendary Irish heroes. This was also the very pantheon that Pearse would aspire to.

Why this should be so about Emmet is instructive in terms of retrospective nationalist mythmaking. As Robert Kee asks in his magisterial three-volume opus, *The Green Flag: A History of Irish Nationalism* (1972): "why exactly the Emmet debacle should have become transformed into a myth of such powerful emotive force, and thus indirectly of political importance, is not immediately easy to see. His failure could hardly have been more ignominious and complete .... Why was it Robert Emmet's portrait above all others that was to go up along with the crucifix in countless small homes in Ireland for over a century and may even be seen there still?" In response, Kee suggests that "The proximity of the crucifix may provide a clue. The success of the Emmet myth lay in the very need to ennoble failure. For tragic failure was to become part of Ireland's identity, something almost indistinguishable from 'the cause' itself" (168–69).

In 1919, Arthur Griffith—the founder of Sinn Fein—wrote an essay on "Nationality," noting: "In the martyrology of history, among crucified nations, Ireland occupies the foremost place" (in Quinlan 111). Recall also the association of Robert Emmet with the crucifix. Indeed, it was at a Robert Emmet Commemoration in 1914 that Padraic Pearse called patriotism "a faith which is of the same nature as religious faith"—and referred to Emmet's hanging as "a sacrifice Christ-like in its perfection" for "such a death always means a redemption." At St. Enda's, he became obsessed with blood-sacrifice, writing that "better is short life with honour than long life with dishonour" and that "I care not though I were to live but one day and one night, if only my fame and my deeds live after me" (Foster, *Modern* 459)—and, famously, that "bloodshed is a cleansing and sanctifying thing". As Foster notes:

> His messianic and sacrificial notion that the "Irish" cause was somehow congruent with Christ's sacrifice appealed to [fellow poets and Rising leaders] MacDonagh and Plunkett as well: the idea of a revolution in consciousness brought about by a symbolic and willed loss of life. Pearse's funeral panegyric on O'Donovan Rossa in August 1915 is correctly seen as its blueprint. "Life springs from death, and from the graves of patriotic men and women spring living nations." (*Modern* 477)

In other words, the very idea of Easter 1916 as a programmed failure had already been scripted in Pearse's mind. (Indeed, the Proclamation itself, read by Pearse on the steps of the General Post Office, invokes "the readiness of [the nation's] children to sacrifice themselves for the common good.") It was hardly coincidence that Easter Sunday was chosen for the rebellion. As Pearse also wrote (in *The Sovereign People*): "The [Irish] people who wept in Gethsemane, who trod the sorrowful way [the Via Dolorosa], who died naked on a cross, who went down into hell, will rise again glorious and immortal, will sit on the right hand of God" (in Quinlan 159). We should note the poignant dramatic irony in Pearse's comments here about Emmet's "Christ-like" sacrifice and about Christ's death and resurrection on Easter Sunday in which, by his own logic, Pearse, who would be himself executed for the Easter Rising, could himself be figured as both Jesus Christ and Robert Emmet. This was not uncanny premonition: this was intentional self-modeling and symbolic gesture. As Charles Townshend writes in his compelling book on *Easter 1916: The Irish Rebellion*: "For Pearse, gesture was all; the only question was how to make the gesture sufficiently striking." The goal (for Pearse, at least[12]) was never successful revolution: the goal was Christ-like martyrology and heroic self-sacrifice.[13]

And of course it worked—but only because the British indeed complied, playing into the hands of Pearse and the rebels by martyring the leaders of the rebellion via 15 quite grisly, and shocking, executions. Had the British not done so, had they given them long prison terms or exiled them to Tasmania or elsewhere (as they had done with Irish rebels for much of the previous century), the at-first very unpopular Rising might not have been retrospectively turned into the powerful, symbolic genesis of the Irish nation. But the aftermath of the Rising, specifically the British decision to execute most of its leaders (over a painfully protracted period), turned national opinion from hostility or ambivalence into nationalist sympathy for, and even worship of, the martyrs of 1916 (Foster notes that "On every level, martyrolatry had taken over"; *Modern* 487)—resulting eventually, 100 years later, in the "massive programme" of commemoration during the recent 2016 centenary celebrations.[14]

*   *   *

Joyce's writing, as I have been arguing, is suffused with matters of national/historical memory and commemoration, anticipating—I have suggested—our contemporary investigations and theories of national memory. Joyce's texts suggest his understanding that what Pierre Nora calls the *lieu de memoire*, the site of historical commemoration—whether it's the equestrian statue of King Billy on College Green or the Wellington memorial or Nelson's Pillar—is a significant cultural battleground over who gets to control the memory of the dead, a space of historical conflict between official, monumental history and subaltern, insurgent memories. What gets remembered historically, what gets forgotten, and why?

What becomes historically consecrated as a marmoreal monument or site or date deserving iconic and official commemoration and celebration?

In other words, how do we remember? How is history remembered and/or forgotten? Why, for example, has the Battle of the Boyne been commemorated for centuries while—as I have previously discussed—the Battle of Aughrim, much more important and decisive a battle, with much greater casualties and consequences, has been largely forgotten or repressed? Just as (in Roy Foster's words) the Boyne "was not an engagement of any great military significance, but it became an encounter of prime symbolic importance" (*Oxford* 152), so also one could argue that—like Emmet's rebellion of 1803—the Easter Rising itself was an event of negligible military importance and effect, but one which—because the British cooperated by martyring its leaders—became an event of immense symbolic significance and consequence.

The traditional Williamite celebrations—such as the eighteenth-century Orange parades on July 1 in Belfast or the marches in Dublin to the equestrian statue of King Billy on College Green—were, as previously noted, state-sponsored commemorations organized by the dominant power, displays and versions of official memory and history centered around monuments and statues celebrating the greatness of the imperial past, what Nietzsche called "monumental history." Post-colonial scholars have distinguished between such official versions of nationalism, which mirror the ideology of British imperialism, "and the subaltern nationalism of the Gaelic underclass, as manifested in nineteenth-century street ballads and agrarian insurgency" (McBride 34).

But the current memorialization of the Easter Rising follows precisely the opposite trajectory: a subaltern, communitarian insurgency that was suppressed and forced into unofficial, demotic memory, eventually becomes transformed—by a post-colonial nation, the Irish Free State, eventually led by one of the leaders of the Easter Rising, Eamon de Valera (the one battalion commander spared from execution—only because he was an American citizen)—transformed into a hallowed moment of official, historical memory (like the Boyne previously, or in US history like the Alamo or like Concord/Lexington), the symbolic first blow of a heroic battle for independence. This is official and historical canonization, and now—after decades of the Republic of Ireland ensconced as the Irish nation—the scope of the 2016 celebrations and commemorations in Ireland was unprecedented.

This was not always so. It is true that, with the creation of the Irish Free State in 1922 and with some of the Rising's survivors (most notably de Valera) later becoming its leaders, the executed leaders of 1916 became increasingly venerated as martyrs; their graves at Arbour Hill were turned into a national monument; the Proclamation was taught in schools as a national document, much like the Declaration of Independence in the USA. In addition to an annual military parade on Easter Sunday in commemoration, the 50th anniversary in 1966 marked a huge national celebration with unabashed pride and pageantry—presided over by President de Valera ("a strangely forlorn and fragile figure as he took the salute from those of his old comrades who remained alive," according to Declan Kiberd, *Inventing* 480). Yet, even as the Rising became increasingly canonized as a key moment in the history of the Irish Republic, the remembering was selective—as its socialist, feminist, and progressive roots were virtually air-brushed out of the official version propagated by the increasingly conservative and Catholic Republic for decades. Then, with the outbreak of the Troubles in Northern Ireland, the official view was further revised and muted—and the Republic of Ireland discontinued its annual parade in Dublin in the 1970s, going so far as to forbid a 1976 commemoration ceremony organized by Sinn Fein and planned to take place at the General Post Office—even as Irish republicans in the North continued to venerate the Rising with murals of its martyrs in Belfast and other Northern towns, and with annual parades on Easter Sunday to compete with the Orange marches in July. But with the IRA ceasefire and the peace process in the 1990s culminating in the Good Friday Agreement in 1998, the official attitude in the South toward the Rising grew more positive again, with an 80th anniversary (1996) ceremony at the Garden of Remembrance in Dublin attended by the Taoiseach John Bruton, and the resumption of the annual military parade in 2006 at the behest of Taoiseach Bertie Ahern. And for the following ten years, the Republic of Ireland went about planning the 1916 Centenary—though, one should note, with more thoughtful awareness now about the blended identities recognized by the still-fragile Good Friday Agreement and its multiple forms of nationalism and inclusiveness on John Bull's other island.

*   *   *

Joyce had anticipated the "hurleystick rebellion" of 1916—but had wanted no part of the bloodshed and blood-sacrifice Pearse's rhetoric and actions both entailed. But Joyce could not have anticipated the results: for just as the widespread success and proliferation of the Roman church came long after the sacrificial martyrdom of Jesus Christ on Good Friday and his resurrection on Easter Sunday, so also the Easter Rising of 1916 has indeed produced—eventually, decades later—the resurrection and results envisioned and planned for by Padraic Pearse.[15]

A final observation: When, on the eve of Easter Sunday 2016, Irish President Michael D. Higgins gave a speech about the legacy of Easter 1916, he called for "a new Ireland"[16]—"We must ensure that our journey into the future is a collective one; one in which the homeless, the migrant, the disadvantaged, the marginalized and each and every citizen … are fellow travelers; a journey which includes all of the multitude of voices that together speak of, and for, a new Ireland"—it seems to me he was not only invoking the logic of the Good Friday Agreement and its broad inclusiveness toward Protestant and Catholic, Unionist and Republican (as well as invoking the current migrant crisis in Europe), but perhaps even echoing an earlier speech and precedent, one in which a fictional Irish Jew gave a parallel stump speech calling, similarly, for a new Ireland, a Nova Hibernia— an Ireland marked by "[u]nion of all, jew, moslem and gentile" in "the new Bloomusalem in the Nova Hibernia of the future" (*U* 15.1685, 1544–45).

NOTES

1. This paragraph has been adapted from chapter 5 of Cheng, *Joyce, Race, and Empire*.
2. Padraig Lenihan, in *1690: Battle of the Boyne*, writes: "Aughrim emphasises the valour and martial qualities of the Jacobites …. This depiction of Jacobites, favourable in many respects, may have been less suitable to Protestant communal rituals in the face of a post-1790s Catholic resurgence" (259).
3. "Forget not the felled! For the lomondations of Oghrem!" (*FW* 340.07–08).
4. We might note that "The Lass of Aughrim" is part of Gretta's memory, after all, because it is *Michael Furey* that Gretta remembers singing the ballad: "It was a young boy I used to know … named Michael Furey. He used to sing that song, *The Lass of Aughrim*. He was very delicate" (*D* 219). So that it is not only Gretta and the Lass herself, but also the repressed memory of Michael Furey, a ghost by absence, who—in Joyce's version of folk memory, here in the form of Gretta's memories—represents that repressed, forgotten, and murdered Irish past, the dead, the bodies of "Men that had fought at Aughrim and the Boyne."

5. From which some of the material in this next section is adapted.

6. Let me note the irony that King Billy died quite unexpectedly in 1702: he was riding and his horse stumbled into a mole's burrow, sending William crashing to the ground and breaking his collarbone; he died of complications soon afterwards. King Billy was, indeed, undone by being blown off his horse.

7. *Ulysses* is a different matter: Hugh Kenner had already in 1982 connected "Cyclops" with 1916: "When the biscuit-tin, by heroic amplification, renders North Central Dublin a mass of ruins we are to remember what patriotic idealism could claim to have accomplished by Easter 1916" (Kenner, *Ulysses*, 139). In the 1990s both Emer Nolan and Enda Duffy read the "Circe" conflagration scene in terms of 1916. More recently, Greg Winston explores the role of 1916 in *Ulysses* in greater detail.

8. As Stephen later notes, "Renan's Jesus is a trifle Buddhistic but the fierce eaters and drinkers of the western world would never worship such a figure. Blood will have blood" (*SH* 190). These words of Stephen's bring to mind Joyce's review in 1903 of a book about Buddhism, in which his sympathy with Buddhist methods of non-aggression and pacifism is clear. After pointing out that "Five things are the five supreme evils for [Buddhists]—fire, water, storms, robbers, and rulers" (note that water, storms, and rulers are things that Stephen fears, too), Joyce goes on to characterize Western values as bellicose and bloodthirsty by contrast: "Our civilization, bequeathed to us by fierce adventurers, eaters of meat and hunters, is so full of hurry and combat, so busy about many things which perhaps are of no importance, that it cannot but see something feeble in a civilization which smiles as it refuses to make the battlefield the test of excellence" (*CW* 94). There is an echo in these thoughts of Stephen, whose only "arms" will be silence, exile, and cunning, and of Joyce, who would—even through two World Wars—steadily refuse to grant the battlefield any validity as a test of worth.

9. The above two paragraphs are adapted from Cheng, "Nationalism, Celticism, and Cosmopolitanism in *A Portrait.*"

10. As Emer Nolan reminds us: "It was a revolution organized by myth-makers and poets: activists who could not even decide on what day the uprising was to take place, and some of whom had to interrupt their rehearsal of a play by W. B. Yeats to participate; insurgents who even forgot to bring the glue to paste up copies of the Proclamation of the Irish Republic" (Nolan, 133).

11. I have previously written about this passage at length, in *Joyce, Race, and Empire*.

12. But certainly not for James Connolly and some of the other 1916 leaders.

13. Pearse wrote, with deliberate prescience, in *The Irish Volunteer* newspaper a year before the Rising: "We have no misgivings, no self questionings … We saw our path with absolute clearness; we took it with absolute deliberateness. We could no other … We go in the calm certitude of having done the clear, clean, sheer thing."

14. As Foster notes further: "The idea that dying for Ireland can be more productive than living for Ireland was enshrined after 1916" (from Episode Three of *1916: the Irish Rebellion*, the University of Notre Dame's documentary film).

15. Note that the commemorations continue to be celebrated on Easter Sunday each year, reinforcing the emphasis on martyrdom, sacrifice, and resurrection via Easter and the liturgical calendar—rather than on April 24 each year, the actual calendar date in 2016 of the Rising (indeed, April 24, 1916 was the *Monday* after Easter).

16. See, for example: http://www.irishtimes.com/news/ireland/irish-news/president-higgins-urges-the-irish-to-continue-building-a-republic-1.2588644; or: http://www.dailymail.co.uk/news/article-3510718/Irish-President-says-not-fully-achieved-dreams-ideals-calls-new-Ireland-nation-marks-birth-100-years-Easter-Rising.html. I would like to thank Gerald McDonough for suggesting this connection.

WORKS CITED

Bhabha, Homi K., ed. *Nation and Narration*. London: Routledge, 1990.

Cheng, Vincent J. *Joyce, Race, and Empire*. Cambridge: Cambridge University Press, 1995.

———. "Nationalism, Celticism, and Cosmopolitanism in *A Portrait*." In *A Portrait of the Artist as a Young Man: Case Studies in Contemporary Criticism*, Second Edition. Ed. R. Brandon Kershner. Boston: Bedford/St. Martin's, 2006. 389–412.

Duffy, Enda. *The Subaltern Ulysses*. Minneapolis: University of Minnesota Press, 1994.

Duffy, Sean. *The Illustrated History of Ireland*. London: McGraw-Hill, 2002.

Ellmann, Richard. *James Joyce*. Revised edition. Oxford: Oxford University Press, 1982.

Encyclopedia Britannica: The New Encyclopaedia Britannica, fifteenth edition, *Micropaedia* vol. 2 (page 448: "Boyne, Battle of the"). Chicago: Encyclopaedia Britannica Inc., 1992.

Foster, R. F. *Modern Ireland 1600–1972*. London: Penguin, 1988.

———, ed. *The Oxford Illustrated History of Ireland*. Oxford: Oxford University Press, 1989.

Gibbons, Luke. *Transformations in Irish Culture*. Cork: Cork Univ. Press, 1996.

———. "'Where Wolfe Tone's statue was not': Joyce, monuments and memory." In McBride 139–59.

Glasheen, Adaline. *Third Census of "Finnegans Wake."* Berkeley: Univ. of California Press, 1977.

Goodby, John, et al. *Irish Studies: The Essential Glossary.* London: Arnold, 2003.

Joyce, James. *Dubliners: Text, Criticism, and Notes,* eds. Robert Scholes and A. Walton Litz. New York: Viking, 1969.

———. *A Portrait of the Artist as a Young Man: Text, Criticism, and Notes,* ed. Chester G. Anderson. New York: Viking, 1968.

———. *Ulysses.* Eds. Hans Walter Gabler et al. New York: Vintage, 1986.

———. *Finnegans Wake.* New York: Viking, 1939.

———. *Stephen Hero.* Eds. John J. Slocum and Herbert Cahoon. New York: New Directions, 1959.

Kee, Robert. *The Green Flag: A History of Irish Nationalism.* London: Weidenfeld and Nicolson, 1972.

———. *Ireland: A History.* Boston: Little, Brown, 1982.

Kenner, Hugh. *Ulysses.* Baltimore, MD: Johns Hopkins University Press, 1987.

Kiberd, Declan. *Inventing Ireland: The Literature of the Modern Nation.* Cambridge, MA: Harvard University Press, 1995.

Leerssen, Joep. "Monument and trauma: varieties of remembrance." In McBride, 204–222.

Lenihan, Padraig. *1690: Battle of the Boyne.* Tempus, 2005.

McBride, Ian, ed. *History and Memory in Modern Ireland.* Cambridge: Cambridge Univ. Press, 2001.

———. "Introduction: memory and national identity in modern Ireland." Introduction to McBride, ed., *History and Memory in Modern Ireland,* 1–42.

McHugh, Roland. *Annotations to "Finnegans Wake."* Baltimore: Johns Hopkins Univ. Press, 1980.

Moore, Thomas. *Moore's Irish Melodies: The Illustrated 1846 Edition.* Mineola, NY: Dover Publications, 2000.

Nolan, Emer. *James Joyce and Nationalism.* London: Routledge, 1995.

Nora, Pierre. *Les lieux de mémoire,* vol. I. Paris: Editions Gallimard, 1997.

Quinlan, Kieran. *Strange Kin: Ireland and the American South.* Baton Rouge: Louisiana State University Press, 2005.

Renan, Ernest. "What Is a Nation?" Trans. Martin Thom. In Homi K. Bhabha, ed., *Nation and Narration.* 8–22.

Rossington, Michael and Anne Whitehead, editors. *Theories of Memory: A Reader.* Baltimore: Johns Hopkins University Press, 2007.

Townshend, Charles. *Easter 1916: The Irish Rebellion.* London: Penguin, 2005.

Whitehead, Anne. *Memory.* New York: Routledge, 2009.

Winston, Greg. *Joyce and Militarism.* Gainesville, FL: University Press of Florida, 2012.

Yeats, William Butler. *The Collected Plays of W. B. Yeats*. New York: Macmillan, 1935.

Yerushalmi, Yosef Hayim. *Zakhor: Jewish History and Jewish Memory*. New York: Schocken Books, 1989.

1916: the Irish Rebellion. Documentary film by the University of Notre Dame's Keough-Naughton Institute for Irish Studies. 2016.

CHAPTER 5

Joyce, Ireland, and the American South: Whiteness, Blackness, and Lost Causes

The previous chapters have had to do, at various times, with James Joyce, with Irish history, and with the American South. These last two chapters will focus on the American South—and its relationship to Irishness.

But what does James Joyce have to do with—or to say about—the American South? How much did Joyce even know about the South? It is not my intention here to rehearse the *influence* James Joyce has had on the South, especially its writers like William Faulkner and F. Scott Fitzgerald—for example, how taken Faulkner was with Joyce's prose, stealing a bootleg copy of *Ulysses* with him on his ill-fated honeymoon, making a pilgrimage to Paris in 1925 and catching glimpses of Joyce in restaurants, and of course modeling his "Faulknerian" prose on Joyce's stream of consciousness. What I would like to do instead, in this chapter, is to put Joyce, Ireland, and the South in conversation with each other: for the results are, as we will see, interesting and suggestive.

*　*　*

I begin this chapter with two moments—one textual, one historical; one well-known to readers of Joyce, one not at all. First the latter:

It is 1877 in Charleston, South Carolina—one of the three Southern cities (along with Savannah and New Orleans) that had the largest and most highly visible concentration of Irish Catholics (while many Scotch

© The Author(s) 2018
V. J. Cheng, *Amnesia and the Nation*, New Directions in Irish and Irish American Literature, https://doi.org/10.1007/978-3-319-71818-7_5

Irish had settled in the South earlier, most of the Irish who came to America in the 19th century were Catholic, many leaving Ireland as a result of the potato famine). It is St. Patrick's Day (actually the day after, since St. Patrick's that year fell on a Sunday). Following their traditional St. Patrick's Day parade in the morning, the Irish reassemble in the afternoon: the place is Hibernian Hall, the landmark of Irish Charleston, home of its Hibernian Society; built in 1841 by architect Thomas U. Walter (who also designed the US Capitol Rotunda), the building still stands today, and is now a recognized national landmark. So a group of prominent Southern Irish Americans assembles there on that March 18, 1877 to commemorate the many young Irish men from South Carolina, North Carolina, and Virginia who had served in the Confederate army during the Civil War—especially Company C of the Charleston Battalion, known as the "Irish Volunteers," who had fought in all the major battles around Charleston, including Secessionville and Battery Wagner, before being sent to fight in Virginia for the rest of the war. (Indeed, six Irishmen rose to become generals in the Confederate Army.)

The purpose of the meeting is to raise money to build a permanent memorial to these Irish confederates in the local Catholic cemetery. In the previous chapter, I had explored the processes of commemoration and memorializing in Irish history and in Joyce's work. The increasingly popular practice in the American South—to memorialize, through statues, plaques, and so on, the bravery of the Confederate soldiers, increasingly portrayed as loyal and selfless martyrs to a noble but doomed cause—was a major part of that revisionist historical movement, begun during Reconstruction, now popularly referred to as the "Lost Cause"—which has greatly shaped and influenced (for better or worse) our popular conceptions—and cultural "memory"—of Southern culture. As David T. Gleeson writes: "Since the Civil War's end, all over the region, white southerners had sought to reinterpret the war effort to their own advantage. Led by organizations such as ladies' memorial associations dedicated to maintaining Confederate cemeteries, they wanted to preserve the memory of the dead, but also their cause, even if it had been a 'lost cause'" ("Another" 53).

But this meeting in 1877 on St. Patrick's was not just a commemoration of the Confederate dead, but clearly also a public display intended to send a message to other white Southerners: we Irish are just like you; we too are loyal Southerners; we too fought in the War; we too believe in the lost cause. The organizers of this gathering wanted to make clear that their memorial would stand for both Irish and Southern causes, reminding contributors of the parallels between the struggles for Irish independence and for Southern independence—by quoting from an address given earlier in

1861, at the start of the War, to the newly formed Irish Volunteers as they were about to go off to war, by the Catholic Bishop of Charleston, Patrick Neison Lynch, a native of County Monaghan: "the banner I present," Bishop Lynch began, "gives to the breeze and the light of the sun the emblems of Erin—the Shamrock and the Harp—with the Palmetto of Carolina and Stars of our Southern Confederacy .... Receive [this flag] then—rally around it. Let it teach you of God—of Erin—of Carolina" (Gleeson, "Another" 51).

God, Erin, and Carolina—an odd trinity, perhaps, but it was the backbone of national faith and identity for these Irish folks in the Southern USA. Indeed, a year later the Irish of Charleston did successfully unveil the permanent monument this meeting had raised money for: a memorial plaque at the top of which stands the Palmetto tree, state symbol of South Carolina, surrounded by shamrocks, Irish Volunteer muskets, and the harp of Erin hanging on the palmetto tree; Irish symbols are thus entwined with those of South Carolina. This unveiling received a lot of attention in the local newspaper, *The News and Courier*, describing the Irish Volunteers as standing "before the people of Carolina the representatives of all that is great and brave and true"—in other words, true Southern patriots, our own boys, no longer just foreigners and immigrants to our shores. In short, the Irish had successfully proven their Southern patriotism and were now an accepted part of Southern white culture. The more interesting question would be: how had these Irish immigrants in the South, within the period of one or two generations, become so Southern—and become accepted as such by native white Southerners? How did the Irish manage to blend their own native identity into a white Southern identity?

Now for the textual moment, a more familiar one to readers of Joyce:

Perhaps the most hilarious and trenchant of the parodies in the "Cyclops" episode of *Ulysses* is the extended account of Robert Emmet's hanging (*U* 12.524–678); I have written about this episode at length elsewhere, but I do want to discuss it briefly here in terms of the dynamics of patriotic martyrdom. An episode earlier, Leopold Bloom had listened to Ben Dollard in the Ormond Bar singing "The Croppy Boy" and had thought about the lines from this song about national heroes and martyrs, about the long list of martyrs sacrificed to the cause: "All gone. All fallen. At the siege of Ross his father, at Gorey all his brothers fell. To Wexford, we are the boys of Wexford, he would. Last of his name and race ... Ireland comes now. My country above the king" (*U* 11.1063–72). When he emerges into the street, Bloom sees "Robert Emmet's last words" in a shop window (and farts while reading them). Now, in "Cyclops," we get a dramatization of Emmet's final moments.

The narrator in the pub tells us that at this point the men "started talking about capital punishment and of course Bloom comes out with the why and the wherefore" (12.450–51), arguing against capital punishment. The discussion then naturally turns to hanging, and to the hanging of the Invincibles, and then to violent revolution and Emmet's hanging; in response to Bloom's attempt at reasoned argument, the Citizen retorts: "—*Sinn Fein! .... sinn fein amhain!* The friends we love are by our side and the foes we hate before us" (12.523–24). The latter sentence is, appropriately, a quotation from a sentimental Thomas Moore song in the *Irish Melodies*—for Moore was instrumental in the sentimentalization and nostalgia of the Irish cause (what Joyce calls here "the Tommy Moore touch"). And now the Citizen and Bloom start "having an argument about the point, the brothers Sheares and Wolfe Tone beyond on Arbour Hill and Robert Emmet and die for our country, the Tommy Moore touch about Sara Curran and she's far from the land" (*U* 12.498–501). These specific references are instructive in terms of the nature of the myth-making of Irish nationalism: in the Rebellion of 1798, the Sheares brothers were both members of the United Irishmen (founded by Wolfe Tone) who were betrayed by an informer; according to the sentimentally popular version of the story, they supposedly went hand in hand to their execution (though there is no real evidence for this version). Sara Curran was secretly engaged to Robert Emmet, who— according to a popular but equally apocryphal legend—was captured when he went to bid her goodbye before fleeing the country; a *very* sentimentalized version of her story was then told by Emmet's old friend (and fellow student at Trinity) Thomas Moore in the *Irish Melodies* ("the Tommy Moore touch"), in a familiar poem titled "She is Far From the Land." (Robert Emmet, hanging, and Thomas Moore all figure prominently in this chapter.) Emmet, of course, as previously noted, was hanged and beheaded on September 20, 1803, after speaking his famous last words ("When my country takes her place among the nations of the earth then and not till then, let my epitaph be written. I have done")— and, as a result of this botched insurrection involving a minor historical figure, has since been raised to the highest mythological pantheon of legendary Irish heroes. (Heroic iconography, holy war, and noble failure—these too figure prominently in this chapter.)

The mythologizing of Robert Emmet is instructive in terms of revisionist nationalist mythmaking, both for Irish nationalism and for Southern nationalism. Indeed, as I will make clear, leading Irish nationalists would play a real role in Southern politics. As we have seen, Robert Kee has noted that "why exactly the Emmet debacle should have become transformed into a myth of such powerful emotive force, and thus indirectly of political importance, is not immediately easy to see. His failure could hardly have been more ignominious and complete .... Why was it Robert Emmet's portrait above all others that was to go up along with the crucifix in countless small homes in Ireland for over a century and may even be seen there still?"—and in response Kee has suggested that "The proximity of the crucifix may provide a clue. The success of the Emmet myth lay in the very need to ennoble failure. For tragic failure was to become part of Ireland's identity, something almost indistinguishable from 'the cause' itself." (Kee, *Green* 168–69). (Indeed, the *Encyclopedia Britannica* describes Emmet as "Irish nationalist leader who inspired the abortive rising of 1803, remembered as a romantic hero of Irish lost causes.")

Tragic failure as part of one's imagined identity—something which, of course, was also being shaped, during the years of Reconstruction, as a central part of the imagined Southern identity. Such sentimental Irish mythmaking, unfortunately, simply reinforces the stage Irish stereotypes so influentially disseminated by Matthew Arnold and others—the Irish as imaginative, creative, romantic, but politically impractical. Basing his ideas on the theories of Ernest Renan, who had found the quintessential Celtic mind to be dreamy and politically ineffectual, Arnold wrote: "The Celtic genius [has] sentiment as its main basis ... with love of beauty, charm and spirituality for its excellence, ineffectualness and self-will for its defect"—a general description still believed by many and still offered up in many contemporary guidebooks. Arnold suggested that the Celt was unduly susceptible to emotion and excitement—"he is truly ... sentimental"—and, with predictable logic, Arnold thus also argued that "the sensibility of the Celtic nature, its nervous exaltation, have something feminine in them, and the Celt is thus peculiarly disposed to feel the spell of the feminine idiosyncrasy; he has an affinity to it; he is not far from its secret" (Arnold 344, 347). This is a kind of "gendered" othering that has similarly been applied to both Jews and to "Orientals," as a way to distinguish them from the sovereign (read: masculine) imperial European subject.

We find elements of such stereotypes of a sentimentalized Irish otherness reflected in, say, the ideas of W. B. Yeats, when he writes of "men born into our Irish solitude, of their curiosity, their rich discourse, their explosive passion, their sense of mystery." Or in the words of another Yeates, contemporary Irish stage actor and director Ray Yeates, writing in a recent collection of essays about the famine: "Deep down ... I think I have always known that to be Irish meant to be a lovable loser" (195); such widespread beliefs echo Renan's and Arnold's ideas of Irish ineffectualness—what Arnold callously referred to as "nations disinherited of political success" in his *On the Study of Celtic Literature*, with its suggestive epigraph from Macpherson's Ossian, "They went forth to the war, but they always fell" (a line which Yeats and others also borrowed). Such images only reinforce an already internalized Irish creed and imagined identity of noble failure and martyrdom, of the nobility in lost causes.[1]

These are, one might note, very similar to some of the stereotypes about Southerners, encouraged by the South itself during its development of the Lost Cause identity: the Southern mindset as romantic, brave, but impractical and reckless—as opposed to a Northern mindset that was shrewd, disciplined, and practical—backed by superior Union resources and numbers. Indeed, advocates of the Lost Cause argue that Confederates were not so much defeated on the battlefield as they were overwhelmed by massive Union resources and manpower; thus, the South was destined to lose from the start, hence a "Lost Cause." (As with the Irish, "They went forth to the war, but they always fell.")

But why did the Irish newcomers in the South fit in so well so quickly? There were of course lots of parallels that naturally made the two groups—Irish immigrants and native white Southerners—feel some shared familiarities. As Sean O'Faolain wrote, comparing his County Cork with Faulkner's rural Mississippi: "there is the same passionate provincialism; the same local patriotism; the same southern nationalism ... The same vanity of the old race; the same gnawing sense of defeat; ... the same escape through sport and drink"; C. Vann Woodward, the great dean of Southern historians, had similarly noted that both Joyce and Faulkner "were conscious of the provinciality of their culture and its subordinate relation to a dominant one" (Quinlan 5).

After all, both Ireland and the South were lands, as Kieran Quinlan notes, "with strikingly similar historical experience[s] of defeat, poverty, and dispossession"; both had fought unsuccessfully for local autonomy, for "home rule" as it were; both have long been thought of as the "problem" (the "Irish problem" and the "Southern problem")—as the romanticized, wild, "untamed peripheries of their respective civilized industrial centers" (Quinlan 4). In comparison with their conquerors, both were backward, agricultural, "semicolonial," and (supposedly) romantic cultures. Both Ireland and the South had histories characterized by defeat and oppression, carrying the sort of Southern "burden" that C. Vann Woodward has shown to be central to the Southern experience—or what in the Irish context Stephen Dedalus calls "the nightmare of history," characterized by an incapacity to forget "old times"—whether "down in the land of cotton" or on the streets of Dublin (as Faulkner quipped, in the South "The past is never dead. In fact, it's not even past"). Both have been much preoccupied with this history of defeat and with intense, sometimes bitter disputes in the interpretation of their pasts (Quinlan 15). In the process, both developed a nationalist myth, using models—as we will see—of religious sacrifice and martyrdom—that became part of their "authentic" identity: the story of a freedom-loving people sacrificed to a lost cause in the face of a superior foreign power, but never giving up the holy struggle for liberation. (As Seamus Deane points out: "All history and literature ... are forms of mythology" [Quinlan 256].)

How do we remember, how do we forget? What do we remember, what do we forget? During Reconstruction, the South developed its own form of revisionist memory/mythology, what is popularly known as the "Lost Cause." The Lost Cause is an interpretation of the Civil War—developed by a number of white Southerners, many of them former Confederate generals or politicians (such as General Jubal A. Early and Confederate President Jefferson Davis)—that, as historian Caroline E. Janney writes, "created and romanticized the 'Old South' and the Confederate war effort, often distorting history in the process. For this reason, many historians have labeled the Lost Cause a myth or legend. It is certainly an important example of public memory, one in which nostalgia for the Confederate past is accompanied by a collective forgetting of the horrors of slavery" (Janney 1). The movement portrayed the South's cause as noble and its leaders as heroic models of old-fashioned chivalry, inevitably defeated by the North's overwhelming numbers and advantages. It resulted in a mania for commemoration and martyrdom that developed "into a type of civil religion ... [with] its own elaborate ceremonies (parades and memorials), icons (statues of Confederate heroes), and 'saints,' especially its 'blessed Trinity' (generals Robert E. Lee and Thomas 'Stonewall' Jackson; and President Jefferson Davis). Confederate cemeteries became places of pilgrimage on the various feast days—to use a Catholic term—of the Confederacy, which included Lee's birthday and the anniversary of Jackson's death" (Gleeson, "Another" 53). Whereas scholars and historians have criticized the Lost Cause as a comforting myth, it continues today to be an important part of how the Civil War is remembered both in the South and in American popular culture (including novels and films). As Janney writes: "The image of African Americans who had been happy under slavery but were overwhelmed by the responsibilities of freedom became widespread and could be found in the fiction of Thomas Nelson Page and Margaret Mitchell, whose novel *Gone with the Wind* won the Pulitzer Prize in 1937. The image also proved particularly useful to white supremacists. In the 1880s and 1890s, white Southerners, decrying 'Yankee aggression' and black 'betrayal,' embarked on an effort to reverse the policies of Reconstruction" (Janney 2).

In brief, the Lost Cause argues six major tenets: (1) That it was secession (and the defense of states' rights), not slavery, that led to the Civil War—for secession was a justifiable response to Northern aggression against the Southern way of life; (2) that black slaves were loyal to their benevolent masters and to the Southern cause, and were neither ready nor eager for the responsibilities of freedom; (3) that the War was lost, in spite of the bravery of the Southern forces, because of the Union's overwhelming advantages: the South was therefore destined to lose from the start, thus a "Lost Cause"; (4) that Confederate soldiers were gallant, heroic, and saintly; (5) that most heroic and saintly of all was Robert E. Lee, a heroic martyr to the cause; and (6) that Southern women were loyal to the Confederate cause and were "sanctified by the sacrifice of their loved ones" (Janney 1).

Lee was portrayed, in Southern iconography, as the ideal of the antebellum Southern gentleman, Christ-like in his selfless virtue and also Christlike in his sacrifice (Janney 4). By focusing on military sacrifice and by depicting slavery as a benevolent institution, the Lost Cause managed to imagine the Civil War as a righteous and holy war in a doomed defense of a beloved Southern way of life, resulting in what Woodward has argued to be a uniquely Southern sense of the tragedy of history. But it is also, one should note, a very Irish one. For the repeated and remarkably seamless association of Robert E. Lee with Christ on the cross (crucified by the Yankees) is also, as we have seen, a very Irish nationalist theme. Recall Arthur Griffith's 1919 essay on "Nationality": "In the martyrology of history, among crucified nations, Ireland occupies the foremost place" (in Quinlan 111). Recall also the association of Robert Emmet with the crucifix. And recall that Robert Emmet Commemoration in 1914, at which Padraic Pearse—who would himself be the martyr of the Easter Rising two years later—called patriotism "a faith which is of the same nature as religious faith"—and referred to Emmet's hanging as "a sacrifice Christ-like in its perfection" for "such a death always means a redemption." In Pearse's estimation, John Mitchel, the Young Irelander hero of 1848, joins Emmet and Wolfe Tone in the pantheon of national heroes, for Mitchel's *Jail Journal,* Pearse noted, was "the last Gospel of the New Testament of Irish nationalism [just] as Wolfe Tone's *Autobiography* is the first." (More on Mitchel later.) As Pearse also wrote (in *The Sovereign People):* "The [Irish] people who wept in Gethsemane, who trod the sorrowful way [the Via Dolorosa], who died naked on a cross, who went down into hell, will rise again glorious and immortal, will sit on the right hand of God" (in Quinlan 159). (Pearse's comments here about Christ's death and resurrection on Easter Sunday are, as noted earlier, rife with poignant irony and premonition—for, by his own logic, Pearse, who would be executed for the Easter Rising in April 1916, could himself be figured as both Robert Emmet and Jesus Christ.) Such a direct relationship between Christ-like martyrology and a nationalist cause, while striking and audacious, would have felt totally comfortable and familiar to Southern lost causers; indeed, novelist Thomas Nelson Page, a leading popularizer and propagator of the Lost Cause, spoke of the South as: "crucified, bound hand and foot; wrapped in the cerements of the grave ... sealed with the seal of the [federal] government ... dead, and buried, and yet she rose again" (in Quinlan 160).

*   *   *

But let us return to that earlier question: Why exactly did the Irish newcomers in the south come to fit in so well so quickly? It is not, I'm afraid, a very pretty story.

For the Irish in the South—both the Scotch Irish who had settled earlier and the Irish Catholics who emigrated in mid-century—were solidly united with native white Southerners on the key political litmus test, "our peculiar institution" of slavery. So that when war broke out, thousands of Irish young men joined the Confederate army and filled brigades of Irish volunteers (a number of which were named after Robert Emmet) all over the South; the War gave them an opportunity to prove to their native neighbors that they belonged and were as Southern as they were, that they were fully behind the cause.

This was not just a matter of proving their Southernness, however. Far from sympathizing with African slaves because they too had experienced a form of slavery back home in Ireland, Irish folk in the American South—it has to be said—fully supported slavery as an institution. Whereas most Irish immigrants were too poor to own slaves (and indeed had to compete with free blacks for jobs on the bottom rung of the economic ladder), they did not oppose the institution. Those that could afford to own slaves, did—including the revered Charles Carroll of the famed Catholic Caroll family in Maryland; indeed, the Irish-born archbishop of New York, John Hughes, was himself a former overseer of slaves in Maryland; many of the Catholic religious orders, both priests and nuns—Jesuits, Capuchins, Ursulines—held slaves (Quinlan 51; see also Chap. 6 of this study).

In this practice, Irish Americans in the South were forcefully and repeatedly criticized back home by the revered Daniel O'Connell, the Liberator, who famously wrote to them (and to the Repeal Associations that had been founded throughout the USA to support his efforts to repeal the Act of Union): "It was not in Ireland that you learned this cruelty. Your mothers were gentle, kind, and humane …. How can your souls have become stained with a darkness blacker than the negro's skin?" In response, many Southern repeal associations chose to either disband or distance themselves from O'Connell; the Repeal Association of Charleston dissolved itself, declaring: "as the alternative has been presented to us by Mr. O'Connell, as we must choose between Ireland and South Carolina, we say South Carolina forever!" (Ignatiev 32) Perhaps the strongest response came from another well-known Irish nationalist, John England, O'Connell's close friend and former colleague (they had agitated together for Catholic Emancipation), a Catholic priest who had since moved to South Carolina and in 1820 had become the first Catholic Bishop of Charleston. Bishop England, writing now as "a Carolinian" from Cork, accuses O'Connell of being ignorant in his criticisms of the South, and that "a more wanton piece of injustice has never been done to a brave and generous people." The aforementioned Bishop Patrick Neison Lynch, also an Irish-born Catholic priest and England's successor as Bishop of Charleston, was so vocal a defender of slavery that in 1864 he was named by President Jefferson Davis to be the Confederacy's delegate to the Vatican (in spite of the fact that Pope Pius IX was strongly opposed to slavery). Lynch composed "one of the last Southern proslavery treatises and the longest published discussion of the institution by a Confederate prelate" (Quinlan 56); he himself, as a bishop, owned 95 slaves.

Unfortunately, even back in Ireland, O'Connell was part of a small minority; he (along with Thomas Moore) stood almost alone in his forceful opposition to American slavery. Arthur Griffith, founder of Sinn Fein, was notoriously racist and pro-slavery. But, while Griffith's views were extreme, they were not atypical. W. B. Yeats was proud of the fact that one of his family's ships had been designed to break the Union blockade. Charles Stewart Parnell felt a romantic sympathy with the South. So did Oscar Wilde, who—during his American speaking tour in 1882—made a pilgrimage to visit Jefferson Davis at his home (and spoke warmly about Davis and Southern culture); on his way there, the train Wilde was riding had to stop temporarily for a lynching which was taking place on the train tracks, an event which did not faze him in the slightest (Quinlan 73).

John England was only one of a number of notable Irish nationalist figures who moved to the South. Several of the Young Irelander leaders of the Rebellion of 1848, and numerous of their followers, also ended up in the South. Irish Southerners welcomed them when they escaped from prisons in Ireland or Australia. Leading rebels William Smith O'Brien (referred to a number of times in *Ulysses*, and whose statue at O'Connell Bridge Bloom notices in "Hades": "Smith O'Brien" in 6.226), Thomas Francis Meagher, and John Mitchel all visited the South to speak and to be welcomed by Irish/Southern hospitality. Smith O'Brien and Mitchel both supported the South in the War Between the States (Meagher did not, and actually became a general in the Union army). A number of Young Irelanders took a particular liking to the South and settled there—most prominently John Mitchel.

Mitchel was, of course, the founder of the *United Irishman* newspaper; after the failed rebellion of 1848, he was sentenced to 14 years of penal servitude in Bermuda and then in Tasmania; while in prison, he wrote his *Jail Journal*, so admired by Padraic Pearse. Eventually Mitchel escaped and settled in America, founding first an Irish Nationalist newspaper in New York (*The Citizen*), then the *Southern Citizen* in Knoxville, TN, and later the powerful *Richmond Enquirer* in Richmond, VA. Joyce mentions Mitchel twice in *Ulysses*: first, the *Jail Journal* is quoted in "Scylla and Charybdis" (12.112); then in "Ithaca," we are told that "In 1885 [Bloom] had publicly expressed his adherence to the collective and national economic programme advocated by ... John Mitchel ... and others, the agrarian policy of Michael Davitt, [and] the constitutional agitation of Charles Stewart Parnell" (17.1645–1649).[2] Mitchel, one of the major figures in the Irish nationalist pantheon, was also the most vocal in his support of slavery. His views were explicitly racist; he believed that "negroes" are "an innately inferior people" and wrote: "We deny that it is a crime, or a wrong, or even a peccadillo to hold slaves, to buy slaves, to keep slaves to their work by flogging or other needful correction. We wish we had a good plantation well-stocked with healthy negroes in Alabama." Mitchel's newspapers became the voice of Irish Southerners, and in them he wrote frequently about both Southern and Irish affairs, always treating the South as the "Ireland of this continent" (Quinlan 71).[3]

In short, the Irish in the South were fully behind the rest of their fellow Southerners in their support of slavery. In recent years, historians of the South and scholars of race and ethnicity have tried to understand *why*. After all, as L.P. Curtis and others have demonstrated, the English had already long equated the Irish with simian apes and with black folks (and, in *Joyce, Race, and Empire*, I have demonstrated Joyce's awareness of these racial dynamics). Now, in America, the Irish were regarded as an in-between race, frequently referred to as "niggers turned inside out"; blacks, for their part, were sometimes called "smoked Irish" (Ignatiev 49). Thomas Nast's famous cartoon in Harper's Weekly (see Fig. 5.1), titled "Black Slaves and White Apes," equates, as equal in political weight, brutish Irish American voters (with simian features) and freed black slaves.

As a result, the Irish immigrant, competing with freed slaves for the most menial jobs, was not automatically considered a white American. The labor competition resulted in frequent bloody riots and violent disputes between Irish immigrants and black workers, both in the North and the South. In the South, Kieran Quinlan suggests, Irish Catholics "were anxious to be identified with southern culture" (51). David Gleeson suggests that Irish immigrants supported slavery because "it made them members of the 'ruling race': their white skin and their acceptance of slavery automatically elevated them from the bottom of southern society" and "through their support for slavery, the Irish gained native respect" (*Irish* 121). In his provocative, controversial, but ultimately convincing book *How the Irish Became White*, Noel Ignatiev goes further, arguing—through a detailed study of American labor history and the resultant violence between the Irish and African Americans—that the Irish in America managed to achieve "whiteness" on the backs of African Americans basically by distinguishing themselves from the blacks they were being racially lumped together with—and they did so by proving to white America that they hated black people more than anyone else, that they could engage in racist violence more than any other immigrant group, and thus that they should no longer simply be thought of as one of the "darker races." In the South, this meant that—through their support of the institution of slavery, through their participation in fighting the War on the Southern side, and through their part in Lost Cause commemoration of their Civil War dead—which is to say that, by performing a newly adapted version of their imagined, Irish "lost-cause" identity—Irish Southerners had gained admission

Fig. 5.1 Thomas Nast cartoon in *Harper's Weekly*, December 2, 1876

(and unquestioned acceptance) as Southern white folks, as part of the "White Republic" (Ignatiev 104), with all the attendant privileges of that designation.

*   *   *

The Lost Cause movement was reflected in many cultural productions, including a number of prominent novels and films that have greatly influenced popular conceptions of the South—such as the novels of Thomas Nelson Page and of Thomas F. Dixon, Jr. The latter's controversial 1905 novel *The Clansman* was then adapted by D. W. Griffith into his highly successful and landmark silent film *The Birth of a Nation* (1915)—a film that inspired the virulent growth and spread of the Ku Klux Klan (see Fig. 5.2). In portraying the emancipated slave as a threat to both democracy and to white womanhood, *The Birth of a Nation* defended white supremacy (in an era when lynching was taking place commonly and unapologetically): in both the book and the movie, the Ku Klux Klan is portrayed sympathetically as upholding the noble traditions of the South and of the Confederacy by defending Southern culture and especially Southern womanhood against the assaults by both freed slaves and Northern carpetbaggers during Reconstruction. (Notably, the newly founded Klan borrowed much of its lore, symbolism, and vestments from Scottish, Irish, and especially Catholic tradition; the novel actually invokes Scottish and Irish history in arguing for Southern rights.)

But perhaps the most influential cultural products of Lost Cause thinking were the spectacularly successful 1936 novel by Margaret Mitchell, *Gone with the Wind*, the bestselling novel of the twentieth century—and the equally popular 1939 film version of her novel. As Janney notes: "until the middle of the twentieth century, and even longer in Virginia, textbooks presented a picture of the Civil War and race relations that owed much to *Gone With the Wind*" (Janney 9). Plantation slaves are sentimentally portrayed as happy members of the family, with affection and loyalty between white masters and black slaves; white Southerners are portrayed as noble, heroic members of a romantic culture tragically destroyed by an unstoppable and destructive force. Notably, the story has, at its very center, an Irish Catholic family (the O'Haras) who own a plantation in Georgia named after the ancient seat of the high kings of Ireland, Tara. There have lately been a number of fascinating scholarly studies on Irishness in *Gone with the Wind*,[4] for in the novel parallels to Irish history are frequently cited

Fig. 5.2 Theatrical poster for *The Birth of a Nation* film (1915)

(Sherman's burning of Atlanta, for example, is compared to Cromwell's massacre at Drogheda), along with frequent references to Robert Emmet, Thomas Moore, and so on; Kieran Quinlan argues, indeed, "that *Gone With The Wind* is far more Irish—and far more Catholic in its references also—than has generally been acknowledged" (129). Margaret Mitchell, herself the daughter of Irish Catholic immigrants, wrote to one of her fans about "the part [we] Irish played in the building up of our Southern section and in the Civil War"—in which "our Southern Irish became more Southern than the Southerners. When the trouble in the 'sixties began [i.e., the War] they went out with the Confederate troops and did great deeds for their new land" (in Quinlan 123). But what is finally most noteworthy is the simple fact that, in the novel's depiction of Southern identity, an Irish Catholic immigrant—Gerald O'Hara—could be accepted as a perfectly natural, unquestioned part of the plantation landscape. As Gleeson points out: "By the 1930s, the essential respectability of Irish southerners had grown to such heights that Margaret Mitchell, herself a descendant of Irish immigrants, was able to create from her ancestry an entirely believable character in [Scarlett's father] Gerald O'Hara" as "a hard-drinking Irish Catholic immigrant ... who hated Orangemen ... and ... became the model patriarch planter." It was now perfectly acceptable to equate Irishness with Southernness: "Thus, the archetypal southern belle in the popular mind, Scarlett O'Hara, was the daughter of an Irish Catholic. The ease with which the public accepted the Irish immigrant and his fictional family as 'true' southerners emphasizes just how well the Irish had blended into the native population" (*Irish* 194). The blending/doubling of a performative, imagined Irish/Southern identity was complete.

*   *   *

Joyce was, in his works, certainly not unaware of the American South, especially as a land being increasingly settled by Irish emigrants—and also as one torn apart by racial strife. Recall that, in *A Portrait of the Artist as a Young Man*, young Stephen Dedalus remembers that "he had heard his father say that [Dante] was a spoiled nun and that she had come out of the convent in the Alleghanies when her brother had got the money from the savages for the trinkets and the chainies" (35). The real-life "Dante" Conway in the Joyce household, Ellmann tells us, never actually made it to America, for she "had been on the verge of becoming a nun in America when her brother, who had made a fortune out of trading with African natives, died and left her 30,000 pounds" (Ellmann II, 25). The fictional Dante's experience at a convent in the South was not unusual: after the South's defeat in the war, the few Irish émigrés to the South were mostly missionary priests and nuns; Quinlan notes that "The recent discoveries of the diaries of two Irish Dominican nuns from comfortable families—but who had probably been sent to America because they didn't have the dowries necessary to support them in their convents at home [nor wealthy brothers, we might add] ... casts a revealing light on contemporary [racist] Irish attitudes" (Quinlan 73).

Joyce certainly couldn't have read *Gone with the Wind* (which came out in 1936) before he wrote *Ulysses* (which came out in 1922)—but it is very tempting to imagine, anachronistically, that he had. For, in one of the most striking and serendipitous coincidences in Joyce's texts, we find in the "Aeolus" chapter a reference to Daniel O'Connell's "monster meetings" at Mullaghmast and at the hill of Tara (where hundreds of thousands gathered to hear him urge repeal of the Union)—here, we find within the same line as the reference to Tara, the phrase "Gone with the wind": "Gone with the wind. Hosts at Mullaghmast and Tara" (*U* 7.880).

But even without reading *Gone with the Wind*, Joyce clearly associated the South, and especially African slavery, with Georgia (in both *Ulysses* and *Finnegans Wake*). In the "Cyclops" episode, soon after the discussion of Emmet's hanging, the men in the pub turn their attention to a newspaper story that features a picture titled: "*Black Beast Burned in Omaha, Ga.*"—a description of a Southern lynching: "A lot of Deadwood Dicks in slouch hats and they firing at a Sambo strung up in a tree with his tongue out and a bonfire under him" (12.1321–28; "lynching," a term associated in Ireland with the "Galway Lynches" [12.1304], was itself evoked just a few lines earlier). Joyce was referring to an actual lynching incident reported in the *London Times*—a story which itself was anachronistic, since this source-incident took place on September 28, 1919 (and thus could not have been in the Dublin papers in 1904): in the reported incident, the black victim had been accused of raping a young white woman; the white lynch mob hanged him, then "riddled his body with bullets, and burned it"; the mob then tried to lynch the mayor for trying to stop the rampage against blacks which ensued. It was the *London Times* that mistakenly reported Omaha as being in Georgia instead of Nebraska; Joyce thus naturally assumed that this racist atrocity took place in Georgia, in the heart of the Deep South.

Indeed, such a lynching incident in the Deep South could well have also come out of the film *Birth of a Nation*—and Joyce certainly knew about both the Griffith film and about the Ku Klux Klan, for there are numerous references in *Finnegans Wake* to both *Birth of a Nation* and to the KKK. For example, at the very beginning of II.3 we find a passage clearly having to do with competing ethnic, racial, and national identities: "it is Hiberio-Miletians and Argloe-Noremen, donated him, birth of an otion that was breeder to sweatoslaves" (*FW* 309.11–12)—with references to Hibernians, Milesians, Norsemen, and Anglo-Normans, all part of the birth of an Irish nation; interestingly, "birth of an otion" is described here as a "breeder" of the "sweat of slaves"—which was certainly true of the American *Birth of a Nation*.[5]

There are a number of passages in *Finnegans Wake* referring to either the KKK (like "Kersse's Korduroy Karicature" in 85.33) or to *Birth of a Nation*. But I would like to conclude this chapter with a brief close reading of the opening page of the *Wake* in terms of the American South and of its black–white dynamics and slavery problem. *Finnegans Wake* begins, of course, with that famous first line describing the topography of Dublin: "riverrun, past Eve and Adam's, from swerve of shore to bend of bay, brings us by a commodius vicus of recirculation back to Howth Castle and Environs." I will discuss the ensuing passage line by line—focusing only on those allusions relevant to my particular topic here, Joyce and the American South.

"Sir Tristram, violer d'amores, fr'over the short sea, had passencore rearrived from North Armorica on this side the scraggy isthmus of Europe Minor to wielderfight his penisolate war." Joyce had written Harriet Shaw Weaver that: "Sir Amory Tristram 1st earl of Howth changed his name to Saint Lawrence, b in Brittany (North Armorica); Tristan et Iseult, passim" (15 November 1926; Ellmann II, 583–84). The name Saint Lawrence further evokes St. Lawrence O'Toole, the first Irish-born Bishop of Dublin, and the patron saint of Dublin. But the name Tristram also conjures up some name-doubles—especially (as Joyce pointed out) the young lover Tristan, who falls in love with the beautiful Iseult or Isolde: in the Arthurian legend (and the Wagner opera), Tristan, one of the knights of the Round Table, was the nephew and heir of King Mark of Cornwall, and was sent to fetch Isolde back from Ireland to wed the king, only to fall in love with her himself. So Tristan would cross "fr'over" (like the "Wild Rover" in the traditional Irish drinking song) the Irish Sea from Brittany, as a "passenger from North Armorica [Brittany]," to get Isolde from Ireland ("Europe Minor"). But this had not yet happened ("passencore" echoes *pas encore*, not yet)—and so we get two different time frames here, doubled. Indeed, the entire passage is about "doubling": both geographically and temporally ("not yet" is the repeated refrain of the passage); Tristram and Tristan; Armorica suggests America. For the Irish people would, in time, be doubled and split up—since in the nineteenth century thousands and thousands would leave the Emerald Isle especially for North America (thus passengers re-arriving in North America), the two lands with the most Irish people in the world. The geographical and temporal doubling is between the Old World and the New World, where millions of Irish folks would be "doubling" the Irish population—that is to say, settling in places like Dublin, Georgia, a town on the Oconee River, in Laurens County, Georgia, first settled by Irish immigrants. This opening page of *Finnegans Wake* indeed anticipates how, in the American South, the Irish would indeed "double" themselves—by blending themselves into "doubled" twins, as white Southerners.

But not yet (*pas encore*), for this had not happened yet: "nor had topsawyer's rocks by the stream Oconee exaggerated themselse to Laurens County's gorgios while they went doublin their mumper all the time." Not yet had someone's rocks exaggerated themselves: which is to say, one's rocks (one's genitals) had not yet grown into an erection; erection leads to sex which leads to procreation, which leads to the doubling of your population, thus doubling your number all the time (with the help of "mum"). Topsawyer's Rock is (believe it or not) an actual rock formation on the Oconee River, in Laurens County, Georgia—or "Laurens County's gorgios"—next to the town of Dublin, Georgia, founded by a Dubliner named Peter Sawyer (the "topsawyer"), a town whose motto is "Doubling all the time." Well, the Irish are indeed doubling all the time: procreating many children, who then move away from Dublin to the American South and start new cities also named Dublin, thus "Doubling their number all the time." From North Armorica (Brittany) to Ireland; from Ireland to North America—the Irish are indeed doubling all the time, creating new "doublins." Likewise, Sir Tristram and St. Lawrence (patron saint of Dublin) get doubled here in "Laurens County"—just as James Joyce exaggerated his own rocks and doubled himself in his son Giorgio (here as "gorgios"). This is pretty amazing stuff.

Let me add that "topsawyer" also echoes, of course, Tom Sawyer. In a book about Irish Finns doubling themselves into Finn-agains, Tom Sawyer and his rival "twin" Huck Finn are Southern American versions of the warring twins, always fighting, like Tristan, for the love of Isolde (or Issy), and fighting to replace their old father figure, King Mark (here, Mark

Twain)—fighting, in other words, to be the "top sawyer." This leads me to ask an intriguing question: in recent years American Studies scholars have speculated on the issue "Is Huck black?" I would like to ask—along with Noel Ignatiev—could Huck also be Irish? After all, Finn is as Irish a name as you could want, and Huck is a sort of Finn-again; as Mark Twain himself wrote about Huck in a letter: "the boy's mouth is a trifle more Irishy than necessary." As Ignatiev notes: "even if Huck's Irishness is pure fancy, it suggests a profound truth about America, that the national character, embodied in the country's most beloved literary figure, is part Irish as well as part Negro" (68–69).

I now skip a couple of sentences and get to the next paragraph: "The fall … of a once wall strait oldparr is retaled early in bed and later on life down through all christian minstrelsy": The story of mankind is, in a sense, a story of doubling—the rise (through one's rocks and erections) and fall of generations. There are a number of versions of the Fall suggested here, including Eden, Babel (the "thunderword"), Tim Finnegan off the Magazine Wall, and—in North America—the Great Fall of Wall Street in 1929 ("the fall … of a once wall strait"): this is a story repeated (retold early in bed and later on life) in the Old World down through all Christian history; in the New World, it is retold through "christian minstrelsy." The Christy Minstrels were, of course, an American blackface minstrel group (led by Edwin Pearce Christy) who famously "performed" Southern slave culture. There has been a lot of fascinating scholarship in recent decades on blackface and on black minstrel shows (including, most recently, surprising arguments by musicologists, in spite of the inherent racism of blackface, that these minstrel shows were popular because they in fact quite accurately portrayed black slave music and dance[6]) and also on the fascinating fact that most of the blackface performers were actually Irish. But what I do want to point out is that Joyce was obviously familiar with this American musical genre. This is clear in *Ulysses*, when in the "Circe" episode Bloom describes a minstrel show: "Eugene Stratton. Even the bones and cornerman at the Livermore christies. Bohee brothers. Sweep for that matter" (15.410–11). Eugene Stratton was a well-known American blackface impersonator playing in Dublin that very night; the Livermore Brothers World Renowned Court Minstrels were also American "christy minstrels" in blackface who had played in Dublin in 1894 and whose show included blackface "cornermen" armed with "bones"; the Bohee brothers were another pair of blackface "christies" who had played Dublin (Gifford, *Ulysses Annotated* 458). Bloom's Circean fantasy now conjures up a typical scene from one of these minstrel shows: "Tom and Sam Bohee, coloured coons in white duck suits, scarlet socks, upstarched Sambo chokers and large scarlet asters in their buttonholes … flashing white kaffir eyes … with smackfatclacking nigger lips" playing their banjos and singing "There's someone in the house with Dina" (15.412–18). Although this is one of Bloom's fantasies, it is also a quite accurate depiction of what minstrel shows like the Livermore Brothers or the Bohee Brothers were in fact like, with their exaggerated and stylized representations of "negro" stereotypes; "white kaffir eyes" refers to G. H. Chirgwin, another music-hall entertainer who "performed in blackface with large white diamonds painted around his eyes, billing himself as the White-Eyed Kaffir" (Gifford 366).

Now back to the first page of the *Wake*: The next sentence describes the fall (the "pftschute") of Finnegan and Finn McCool in Phoenix Park, by the Castle Knock gate ("at the knock out in the park") "where oranges have been laid out to rust upon the green since devlinsfirst loved livvy": ever since Dubliners have first loved the river Liffey, there have been ethnic, racial and religious rivalries, enmities, hatred, and wars—for the hatred between the orange and the green has resulted in many bodies being laid out to rest in the green cemeteries of Ireland. What now follows is a paragraph about bitter wars and hatreds between rival groups competing for dominance: "What clashes here of wills gen wonts, oystrygods gaggin fishygods! Brekkek Kekkek Kekkek Kekkek! Koax Koax Koax! Ualu Ualu Ualu! Quaouauh!" There are many clashes and battles in this paragraph— "wills" against "wonts," oyster gods against fishy gods, Ostrigoths against Visigoths (in the Battle of Catalaunian Fields)—followed by what I take to be (via Aristophanes's *The Frogs*) the sounds of battle, or battle cries: but notice that these battle cries—Kekkek Kekkek Kekkek! Koax Koax Koax!— repeatedly suggest KKK—for the central racial rivalry and ethnic violence in the Irish New World, in the world of Dublin, GA, is that between black and white, between black slaves and the white boys of the Klux Klan. Indeed, in the very next sentence we get a number of versions of these competing twins (like Tom and Huck) fighting to replace old King Mark Twain: "Where the Baddelaries partisans are out to mathmaster Malachus Micgranes and the Verdons catapelting the camibalistics out of the Whoyteboyce of Hoodie Head. Assiegates and boomeringstroms." There are many weapons being used here in the midst of a "Baddel" between partisans: a badelaire is a type of sword; Ares is the god of War; a partisan is a type of lance; a malchus is a type of sword; a verdun is a type of lance, as well as the Battle of Verdun; catapults and ballistics are also here. And the partisans themselves are Shem and Shaun in the form of Stephen Dedalus and Buck Mulligan, for we have one partisan from Baudelaire's Paris ("Baddelaries partisans") trying to master the other, Malachi Mulligan. "Camibalistics" and "boomeringstroms" also suggest black cannibals, and we have racial issues between blacks and whites again—not only in colonial Africa (assegais are African spears), but also in Australia between white settlers and aborigines (boomerangs are used as weapons by aborigines Down Under)—and most notably also in the land of the KKK and Dublin GA: "Whoyteboyce of Hoodie Head" recalls not only the "White Boys," eighteenth-century Irish insurrectionists dressed in white shirts, but of course the white boys with hooded heads of the KKK. Orange versus Green, Protestant versus Catholic, European versus African, Aussie versus Aborigine, and Klansman versus black slave: Joyce is lamenting all these forms of internecine violence and hatred.[7]

All of this senseless hatred and killing of one's own countrymen and brothers must have appalled the pacifist Joyce. Or so I read the next sentence: "Sod's brood, be me fear! Sanglorians, save! Arms apeal with larms, appalling. Killykillykilly: a toll, a toll." All this killing is enough to make one want to swear: "God's blood! by my faith"—but also the blood shed by Irishmen, "Sod's brood"—the brood of Ireland, the "Old Sod" (as well as the old Sow who eats her brood). St. Lawrence, save us! ("Sanglorians, save!")—for there is no real glory in all this killing (*sans* glory), only blood (*sang* in French) and tears (*sanglots* in French). All this war and killing and hatred ("Killykillykilly": KKK again) involves guns ("arms") and a lot of noise (*Lärm* in German) full of the "peal" of bells, knelling the toll of death ("a toll, a toll") and for whom the bell tolls. (Australia is here again in "atoll," perhaps referring to the atolls of "New Ireland" in New Guinea). It is indeed "appalling"—for we should raise our arms in a tearful appeal for peace: "Arms apeal with larms, appalling" (*larmes* is French for tears), as we contemplate the toll of death and for whom the bell tolls.

This pacifist appeal about the human cost of war and violence—that is, death and blood without glory—is, to my mind, one of the most moving passages in *Finnegans Wake*. And Joyce's two prime examples of this cost are the violence of orange versus green and of black versus white, the killing between Irishmen of Orange and Green persuasions—and the killing of blacks, so long equated racially with the Irish, by the white boys in hooded heads of the Ku Klux Klan—in that New Ireland of the New World, in the new Irish "doublins" in places like Laurens County, Georgia. The doubling of their number all the time—that is, the twinning of the

Irish in the New World, in the American South—not only re-performs the "lost-cause" identity of Irishness, but re-produces a New World version of internecine ethnic/racial warfare. A toll, a toll indeed.

NOTES

1. We still see traces everywhere of such beliefs in a brooding, ineffectual, dreamy Irish spirit. The Irish American editor of *Irish Hunger*, Tom Hayden (he of sixties-activism fame and Jane Fonda's ex-husband) writes about the dark and brooding Robert F. Kennedy as "a raw Celtic spirit" who made him realize that "there was such a thing as an Irish soul" (Hayden 287). Even in contemporary Irish cultural studies we find the continued traces of the reification of Irish otherness, as in Terry Eagleton's description of Irish writing as "the home of a brooding, isolated subjectivity confronting a recalcitrant world" (18). (The previous page has been adapted from material in Cheng, *Inauthentic: The Anxiety over Culture and Identity.*)

2. Julieann Ulin has recently noted the greater presence of Mitchel's ideas in *Ulysses*, especially in "Cyclops," and has even suggested that he might have been Joyce's model for the "Citizen" (Ulin 26).

3. All three of Mitchel's sons fought in the Confederate army: his youngest son was killed in Pickett's division at Gettysburg; another son was killed a year later as commander of Fort Sumter; a third lost an arm in battle (Quinlan 83).

4. See, for example, Geraldine Higgins's essay "Tara, the O'Haras, and the Irish *Gone with the Wind.*"

5. Another odd serendipity/coincidence is that, in 1914, a year before *Birth of a Nation* came out, Griffith released a movie called *The Escape*, which Lillian Gish (the star of *Birth of a Nation*) recalled as one of the finest films Griffith ever made. Unfortunately, there are no surviving copies of this silent film, and it is now considered a lost film: but the lead character in the film's story is called—of all things—Jim Joyce.

6. See, for example: Christopher J. Smith, "Blacks and Irish on the Riverine Frontiers: The Roots of American Popular Music."

7. There is something quite perceptive in Joyce's connection between the White Boys and the Klan. Ignatiev notes: "The Irish tradition of labor organization goes back to the Defenders of 1641, the earliest known example of a secret society in Ireland. In the eighteenth century there appeared the Whiteboys, so called because its members wore white shirts over their clothes as a disguise. Other names were Molly Maguires, Levellers, and Right Boys" (107). Furthermore, Irish historian Alvin Jackson has pointed out that the Orange Order has an iconography derived from religion that is very much like that of the KKK (in Quinlan 160). The Klan, of course, borrowed much

of its lore and symbolism from Irish and Scottish traditions (and its vestments from the Catholic Church). Indeed, Thomas Dixon's 1905 novel *The Clansman* invoked Scottish and Irish history in arguing for white Southern rights (Quinlan 116–117).

WORKS CITED

Arnold, Matthew. "On the Study of Celtic Literature." 1910. *English Literature and Irish Politics*, vol. 9 of *The Complete Prose Works of Matthew Arnold*. Ed. R. H. Super. Ann Arbor: University of Michigan Press, 1973.

Cheng, Vincent J. *Joyce, Race, and Empire.* Cambridge: Cambridge University Press, 1995.

———. *Inauthentic: The Anxiety Over Culture and Identity.* New Brunswick, NJ: Rutgers University Press, 2004.

Eagleton, Terry. "Form and Ideology in the Anglo-Irish Novel." *Bullan* 1.1 (1994): 17–26.

Ellmann, Richard. *James Joyce.* Revised edition. Oxford: Oxford University Press, 1982.

Gifford, Don, and Robert J. Seidman. *"Ulysses" Annotated: Notes for James Joyce's "Ulysses."* Revised edition. Berkeley: University of California Press, 1988.

Gleeson, David T. *The Irish in the South, 1815–1877.* Chapel Hill: University of North Carolina Press, 2001.

———. "Another 'Lost Cause': The Irish in the South Remember the Confederacy." *Southern Cultures* 17.1 (Spring 2011: *The Irish*): 50–74.

Hayden, Tom, ed. *Irish Hunger: Personal Reflections on the Legacy of the Famine.* Boulder: Roberts Rinehart; Dublin: Wolfhound Press, 1997.

Higgins, Geraldine. "Tara, the O'Haras, and the Irish *Gone with the Wind*." *Southern Cultures* 17.1 (Spring 2011: *The Irish*): 30–49.

Ignatiev, Noel. *How the Irish Became White.* New York: Routledge, 1995.

Janney, Caroline E. "The Lost Cause." *Encyclopedia Virginia.* Ed. Brendan Wolfe. 8 Jan. 2013. Virginia Foundation for the Humanities. 9 May 2011: http://www.EncyclopediaVirginia.org/Lost_Cause_The

Joyce, James. *A Portrait of the Artist as a Young Man: Text, Criticism, and Notes*, ed. Chester G. Anderson. New York: Viking, 1968.

———. *Ulysses.* Eds. Hans Walter Gabler et al. New York: Vintage, 1986.

———. *Finnegans Wake.* New York: Viking, 1939.

Kee, Robert. *The Green Flag: A History of Irish Nationalism.* London: Weidenfeld and Nicolson, 1972.

Moore, Thomas. *Moore's Irish Melodies: The Illustrated 1846 Edition.* Mineola, NY: Dover Publications, 2000.

Quinlan, Kieran. *Strange Kin: Ireland and the American South.* Baton Rouge: Louisiana State University Press, 2005.

Smith, Christopher J. "Blacks and Irish on the Riverine Frontiers: The Roots of American Popular Music." *Southern Cultures* 17.1 (Spring 2011: *The Irish*): 75–102.

Ulin, Julieann. "'Famished Ghosts': Famine Memory in James Joyce's *Ulysses*". *Joyce Studies Annual* 2011: 20–63.

Yeates, Ray. "My Famine." In Hayden, *Irish Hunger* 191–200.

Yeats, William Butler. *The Collected Plays of W. B. Yeats*. New York: Macmillan, 1935.

CHAPTER 6

Slavery, the South, and Ethical Remembrancing

The Emanuel African Methodist Episcopal (AME) Church in Charleston, South Carolina, founded in 1816, is the oldest AME church in the South, housing the oldest black congregation south of Baltimore, Maryland. Charleston, of course, was—in the eighteenth and nineteenth centuries—the center of white aristocratic, slave-owning Southern culture, the center of a robust slave trade (its Old Slave Mart still stands), the city that initiated the Civil War (with the shelling of Fort Sumter), the proud cultural capital of the state that was the cradle of Secession. Located just a short walk from Hibernian Hall, the center (as discussed in the previous chapter) of Irish and Irish American culture in South Carolina (including Irish support of the Confederacy), "Mother Emanuel"—as the Emanuel AME church is affectionately known in Charleston—itself has a long history of involvement in issues surrounding slavery and the Civil War. In 1821 one of the church's founders, Denmark Vesey, organized a major slave uprising in Charleston, but authorities were tipped off before it began. The planned revolt, however, resulted in mass hysteria among white culture throughout the South. Vesey and 35 other slaves were executed, and the AME church was burned. It was finally rebuilt in 1834 (and, like Hibernian Hall, is today listed as a historic building by the National Park Service). After the war, it has continued to be a center for black issues—hosting civil rights marchers and pulpit speakers that have included Booker T. Washington and Martin Luther King, Jr.

© The Author(s) 2018   119
V. J. Cheng, *Amnesia and the Nation*, New Directions in Irish and Irish
American Literature, https://doi.org/10.1007/978-3-319-71818-7_6

On the evening of June 17, 2015, a 22-year-old white male named Dylann Storm Roof entered Mother Emanuel and asked to join a Bible study group taking place inside. He was welcomed into the group. But, after about an hour, Roof pulled out a gun and opened fire—killing nine people, all African American, including the Rev. Clementa Pinckney, the church's pastor and a South Carolina state senator—while saying as he began shooting, according to witnesses, that "I have to do it. You rape our women and you're taking over our country. And you have to go" (Jenkins 1; Roof had also told a friend, prior to the shooting, that he "wanted to start a civil war"). As a shocked country mourned, President Barack Obama came to Charleston to deliver a eulogy for Rev. Pinckney. Meantime, Roof was discovered to have posted on his personal website a racist, white supremacist manifesto (of nearly 2500 words) targeting blacks, Jews, and Hispanics, saying: "I have no choice. I am not in the position to, alone, go into the ghetto and fight. I chose Charleston because it is most historic city in my state, and at one time had the highest ratio of blacks to Whites in the country. We have no skinheads, no real KKK, no one doing anything but talking on the internet. Well someone has to have the bravery to take it to the real world, and I guess that has to be me" (*New York Times* June 20, 2015).

In December 2016 Dylann Roof was convicted in Federal Court of 33 capital hate crimes, and in the following month was given the death sentence. But in the intervening time, the Mother Emanuel massacre—its circumstances and its motivations—has, as we will see, reignited all sorts of difficult questions having to do with race, remembering, forgetting, and commemoration.

*   *   *

Let's first return for a moment to Yosef Yerushalmi's key question: "[G]iven the need both to remember and to forget, where are the lines to be drawn? … How much history do we require? What kind of history? What should we remember, what can we afford to forget, what must we forget?" (Yerushalmi 107). In other words, what should we forget, and what should we remember? And *when* should we forget, and when remember?

Recall that Ernest Renan had argued for the importance of forgetting for the sake of maintaining national unity: "Yet the essence of a nation is that all individuals have many things in common; and also that they have forgotten many things. No French citizen knows whether he is a Burgundian, an Alan, a Taifale, or a Visigoth, yet every French citizen has to have forgotten the massacre of Sa[i]nt Bartholomew, or the massacres that took place in the Midi in the thirteenth century." For, as he notes, "Unity is always effected by brutality." So, for the purposes of national harmony, "it is good for everyone to know how to forget" (Renan 15–16).

Yet the question arises, as I argued earlier, whether such collective amnesia can be permanent, or whether—as with repressed memories in trauma victims, or as arguably with the cycles of genocidal violence during the 1990s in Bosnia and Croatia—there will at some point emerge a return of the repressed. One might ask similar questions about the American Civil War: should we all bury the hatchet and forget the past, as it were, and accept that we are now one unified, indivisible nation? Or is that merely a form of repression for a Southern culture in which the past "is never past?" As Pulitzer Prize-winning journalist Tony Horwitz writes in *Confederates in the Attic: Dispatches from the Unfinished Civil War* (5–6):

> During the previous decade, I'd worked as a foreign correspondent in lands where memories were elephantine: Bosnia, Iraq, Northern Ireland, Aboriginal Australia. Serbs spoke bitterly of their defeat by Muslim armies at Kosovo as though the battle had occurred yesterday, not in 1389. Protestants in Belfast referred fondly to "King Billy" as if he were a family friend rather than the English monarch who led Orangemen to victory in 1690.

But when he returned to America, Horwitz was struck by the contrast: "[F]ew things felt stranger than America's amnesia about its past"—in a culture in which, according to a government survey, 93 percent of American students couldn't identify what "important event" occurred in Philadelphia in 1776, and 73 percent of adults could not identify what "D-Day" signified (6). Yet, as Horwitz notes, the exception was that "Americans remained obsessed with the Civil War"—not by way of history books but by way of popular culture: "Ken Burns's TV documentary on the Civil War riveted the nation for weeks" and "*Glory* and *Gettysburg* played to packed movie houses" (5).

Indeed, this has been the case for over a hundred years: the "Lost Cause" interpretation of the Civil War has been (and continues to be) maintained and sustained not by history books (most of which decry the Lost Cause movement) but rather by cultural production, including a number of prominent novels and films recirculating the Lost Cause logic— in which nostalgia for the antebellum past merges with a collective amnesia about the horror of slavery, portraying the South's cause as noble and its leaders as heroic models of old-fashioned chivalry, inevitably defeated by the North's overwhelming numbers and advantages. These ideas were promoted by many cultural productions, including a number of prominent novels and films—such as the novels of Thomas Nelson Page and of Thomas F. Dixon, Jr.—including the latter's controversial 1905 novel *The Clansman* which was then adapted by D. W. Griffith into a highly successful and landmark silent film, *The Birth of a Nation* (1915). The two most influential cultural products of Lost Cause thinking were, however—as I pointed out in the previous chapter—the spectacularly successful 1936 novel by Margaret Mitchell, *Gone with the Wind*, and the equally popular 1939 film version of her novel. As Caroline Janney writes: "The image of African Americans who had been happy under slavery but were overwhelmed by the responsibilities of freedom became widespread and could be found in the fiction of Thomas Nelson Page and Margaret Mitchell, whose novel *Gone With The Wind* won the Pulitzer Prize in 1937. The image also proved particularly useful to white supremacists. In the 1880s and 1890s, white Southerners, decrying 'Yankee aggression' and black 'betrayal,' embarked on an effort to reverse the policies of Reconstruction." Even today, contemporary textbooks can still be found presenting "a picture of the Civil War and race relations that owed much to *Gone With the Wind*" (Janney 2, 9)—in which plantation slaves are sentimentally portrayed as happy members of the family, and white Southerners are portrayed as noble, heroic members of a romantic culture tragically destroyed by an unstoppable and destructive force.

Popular culture fueling a nostalgia which distorts the realities of the past: this is, as I have noted in previous chapters, a form of "remembering" that itself is actually a version of amnesia and forgetting, one which (as we have seen) James Joyce repeatedly decries in his works. But this sort of popular culture–induced nostalgia and distortion are still very much at work in America today: consider the recent children's picture book *A Birthday Cake for George Washington*, published in January 2016: George Washington is depicted amidst his happy slaves, in a narrative presenting upbeat and sentimentalized images of Washington's cook Hercules and his daughter Delia—while neglecting the evils of slavery and the fact that Hercules tried, and eventually managed, to escape. The understandable furor and controversy that ensued following the book's publication forced its publisher, Scholastic, to withdraw it from the market altogether (*Salt Lake Tribune* January 19, 2016, A2). Or consider the monster-hit Broadway musical "Hamilton," a hip-hop interpretation of Alexander

Hamilton's life, which received the 2016 Pulitzer Prize for Drama. In spite of the innovative music and the multiethnic cast, historians have pointed out that the musical presents a rose-tinted view of the nation's founders and glorifies Hamilton by overstating his opposition to slavery while turning a blind eye to the less attractive views he held—such as his unabashed elitism, his mistrust of the masses, and his support for a monarchical form of government. Indeed, Hamilton actually married into a very wealthy, slaveholding family (the Schuylers)—and was more interested in elitist economics than in fighting slavery (see *New York Times* April 11, 2016, A1, A10). As National Public Radio reporter Cokie Roberts notes about this airbrushed version of Hamilton's life:

> It's curious that Alexander Hamilton, who so aspired to join the establishment, is arousing such a passionate defense in these populist times. All he ever wanted was to be "in." And he found the perfect way—through his wife. He joined two of the most revered families of Dutch New York when he wed Elizabeth Schuyler, whose mother was a Van Rensselaer. (*New York Times* April 20, 2016, A23)

Ironically, the success of this musical about our first Secretary of the Treasury was so huge that his recent successor, Treasury Secretary Jacob J. Lew, decided to keep Hamilton's image on the front of the $10 bill—instead of replacing him with a woman, long expected to be Harriet Tubman, an abolitionist and former slave, as had been originally planned. Thus does white male glorification eclipse black slave heroism, and thus does popular culture shape and influence our attitudes towards our race history—whether it is slavery, the Civil War, or contemporary race relations.

Indeed, we might argue that *this* is how Americans get their history nowadays: in the case of the Civil War, through popular cultural productions—not only Ken Burns's documentary (which, after all, requires many hours of intellectual stamina), but especially the recent remake of Alex Haley's *Roots*, or recent films like *Lincoln, 12 Years a Slave, Cold Mountain*, and so on. The result—however well-meaning—can be a distorted nostalgia not unlike the versions of "imperialist nostalgia" that late-twentieth-century British culture indulged in vis-à-vis the British Raj in India (think of films and television series like *Jewel in the Crown, Heat and Dust, Passage to India*, and so on, and the more recent television series *Indian Summers*) and that Americans continue to indulge in vis-à-vis Native Americans (think of *Dances with Wolves, Billy Jack*, and so on)—sentimentalizing the natives and then identifying with them (and with Navajo art, and so on) now that we have largely destroyed their culture. In spite of the fact that works like *Jewel in the Crown* and *Dances with Wolves* are artistically effective and ideologically sensitive and well-meaning, the audience nevertheless is given the opportunity to indulge in the experience (and *frisson*) of reliving a period when "we" still ruled the world, and to indulge in a conscience-salving sympathy for (and even identification with) a sentimentalized version of the natives and the native culture that "we" happen to have already largely destroyed (and which seems doomed to extinction in the face of modernity anyways). Such nostalgia is not harmless: indeed, Lost Cause works like *Birth of a Nation* and *Gone with the Wind*, in both novelistic and cinematic forms, resulted in providing legitimacy—as well as a huge increase in membership—for the Ku Klux Klan and its racist activities, from segregation to cross-burning to lynching. Revisionist/imperialist nostalgia about the past also allows for a whitewash of past misdeeds: in the case of the Lost Cause, that the War was fought only to defend our sovereignty from northern incursion and was really not at all about slavery (since our darkies were perfectly happy in the fields as part of a plantation system that treated them quite humanely); so let's continue to indulge in thinking about "When We Were Still Great" (Tony Horwitz chronicles how the Lost Cause is alive and well in the South, where for many the Civil War never ended but where "They think it's still half-time"; 22). This is a logic that runs parallel to the revisionist nostalgia of contemporary right-wing parties in Germany and Japan, fantasizing a return to a "pure" national culture (before we lost our greatness to migrants and foreigners), a logic parallel to the one that earlier had swept Hitler into power; thus, they can fantasize that what they did (in World War II) was for defensible reasons which were not really so bad—a logic which of course leads right into phenomena like Holocaust denial or the Japanese denial about committing atrocities (in Nanjing, or with Korean comfort women). Donald Trump's successful "Make America Great Again" campaign worked on precisely the same nostalgic/sentimental distortion: let's return to that time when everything made sense and was simple and good and the world bowed before us and we were all prosperous, happy, and white—never mind the fact that there never was such an idealized time and that instead we actually had rampant sexism and misogyny and homophobia, the murders of Civil Rights marchers, race riots in Watts, the assassinations of John Kennedy, Robert Kennedy, Martin Luther King Jr., the Vietnam War, Watergate, and so on. The "Make America Great Again" logic and the accompanying whitewashing of the past is most appealing to, and most effective, with a disaffected white underclass feeling threatened by foreigners, immigrants, and migrants—and explains in part Trump's publicly stated admiration for tyrants and autocrats like Saddam Hussein, Vladimir Putin, and even Hitler. More importantly: such a logic can foster and result directly in contemporary racist hatred, violence, and terrorism—as is clear in the resulting case of Dylann Roof and the Mother Emanuel massacre.

*   *   *

During the investigations in the wake of the Mother Emanuel massacre, police found that Dylann Roof had posed for photographs with a Confederate rebel flag in his hand (Fig. 6.1) and a Confederate flag on his car's license plate. A symbol of the antebellum South reviled by African Americans as the prime banner of racist, pro-slavery hatred, the rebel flag is a hallowed icon and source of inspiration for both Lost Cause Southerners and for white supremacist hate groups. In the wake of the massacre, South Carolina's Republican Governor Nikki Haley urged state lawmakers—in a

Fig. 6.1 Dylann Roof and Confederate flag

reversal of her own previous position on the issue—to pass legislation to finally remove the Confederate battle flag still flying over the South Carolina Statehouse, finally acknowledging that for many people "the flag is a deeply offensive symbol of a brutally oppressive past" (Hemmer 2); and the legislature did indeed remove the flag later that summer. So that a few months later, on Martin Luther King Day on January 19, 2016, civil rights leaders from across the nation gathered at the South Carolina Statehouse to pay homage to Reverend King—for the first time without the Confederate flag hovering over them and mocking their efforts. Three Democratic presidential candidates—Hillary Clinton, Bernie Sanders, and Martin O'Malley—also spoke at the celebration. But only Clinton made specific reference to the Confederate flag, praising Haley and the Republican legislature for working with the NAACP in the wake of the shootings and for choosing to remove the symbol that had inspired Dylann Roof: "We couldn't celebrate [King] *and* the Confederacy. We had to choose." Clinton added: "And South Carolina made the right choice" (*Salt Lake Tribune* January 19, 2016, A5).

Was it the "right choice?" The Mother Emanuel church killings have reignited a passionate debate across the nation, especially in the Southern states, about the symbols and monuments of the Confederacy and about how to properly honor and commemorate the past. After all, should we not allow white Southerners to honor and feel pride in their own history and local traditions? Or should we be sensitive instead to the feelings of a long-suffering people and remove the symbols of an oppressive past—and, in the process, thus perhaps remove/erase/deny historical artifacts and realities, and distort historical memory? Isn't such removal/erasure just a politically correct and well-meaning version of the airbrushing of history that Kundera was so critical of? But don't such symbols also simply continue to stoke anger and national dissension, reminding African Americans— as also with the Orange marches during marching season in Belfast—of their inferior social and class status while motivating and inspiring white supremacist hate groups? We are back to Renan's observation that unity was always achieved through brutality, and that for the sake of national unity it is perhaps good for everyone to be able to forget; we do not want to keep fighting ancient battles between Visigoths, Alans, Taifales, and so on. We want to be able to move on, to have reconciliation and unity. But what Renan said might be true of modern-day France, where no French citizen remembers or cares anymore whether he or she is of Visigoth, Alan, or Taifale, ancestry. Such forgetting can safely occur when the brutalities of the past are distant and unlikely to rise again, like the undead, from the grave. But for African Americans, the wounds of slavery are still very raw and fresh—in view of the continuing legacies of slavery and racial prejudice in this country. And, obviously, for many white Southerners, too, the past is clearly not yet past—and the Civil War is itself still quite raw. In South Carolina, as Jack Jenkins writes about his home state, "support for the Confederate flag still runs deep …. this is where reenactments of the 'War of Northern Aggression' are a regular occurrence, little league teams are sponsored by the Sons of Confederate Veterans, and school children are encouraged to participate in essay contests glorifying Robert E. Lee." The Confederate flag, they argue, is a proud symbol passed down from generation to generation that "has more to do with barbecues and pickup trucks than with slavery or racism," a symbol that "[is] about heritage, not hate" (Jenkins 3).[1]

In the wake of the racially motivated killings at the Mother Emanuel Church in Charleston, state governments and universities across the country have been struggling with, and reevaluating, their own displays of Confederate symbols. In Kentucky, the University of Louisville and the city of Louisville decided (in Spring 2016) to remove a large Confederate monument, built in 1895, near the University campus. But Kentucky, as the birthplace of both Abraham Lincoln and Jefferson Davis, the two opposing Presidents of the Union and the Confederacy during the War, claims both men as native sons, and both are honored with statues in the state Capitol Rotunda. After the Charleston church shootings, leaders of both parties in the Kentucky legislature called for the removal of the statue of Davis. But a state commission voted 7-2 to let it stay (*Salt Lake Tribune* May 1, 2016, A8).

The Mother Emanuel killings in South Carolina, committed by a killer who had photographed himself proudly with the Confederate flag, resulted in national outrage about the flag's presence and role in inciting hate crimes, along with other confederate symbols; indeed, the Southern Poverty Law Center reports that there are at least 1170 such publicly funded Confederate monuments and symbols in our country. What should we do with such problematic symbols? Within a week after the killings in Charleston, the Governor of Alabama, Robert Bentley, had the four Confederate flags outside the State Capitol in Montgomery removed without further debate. Several cities in Mississippi refused to fly the Mississippi state flag, the one remaining state flag still carrying the Confederate emblem. Walmart and other stores stopped selling merchandise carrying the battle flag, as Confederate symbols were increasingly removed from view.

But there has since been a backlash, and the momentum to remove such reminders of the Confederacy has stalled. Confederate symbols and flags again began selling, more briskly than ever, at retail stores. In a number of states, state legislatures have been trying to legally protect and authorize displays of pride in the Confederate heritage. Tennessee and Alabama proposed bills to protect controversial memorials and monuments, even as Virginia Governor Terry McAuliffe vetoed a similar bill in his state. State Senator Gerald Allen of Alabama, in proposing a bill to prohibit such monuments from being "relocated, removed, altered, renamed or otherwise disturbed" without legislative approval, commented: "[W]hen the governor did what he did [that is, remove the Confederate flags in front of the state capitol], it just punctuated the fact that we can't erase history, we can't whitewash it or push it under the carpet like it never happened" (*New York Times* March 14, 2016, A10). But is removing a symbol that incites racist hatred and violence the same as erasing or whitewashing history? Jenkins reminds us that, in actuality, it is the Confederate flag itself (and not its removal) that has encouraged Lost Cause historical revisionism and whitewashing:

> It doesn't matter how many times you tell the average Confederate flag-waver that, yes, the Civil War *was* about slavery—specifically the state's right to own slaves—because leaders of South Carolina said as much in their own articles of secession back in 1860, which mentioned slavery no fewer than 18 times. It doesn't matter how delicately you explain that this fact makes the flag inherently offensive to African Americans, because it represents a time when South Carolina was willing to go to war just to retain the right to own people as property. It also doesn't matter how fervently you insist that after the war, the flag was consistently used as a rallying cry for racists, with Klan members, vigilantes, and segregationists waving it proudly as they beat, terrorized, and murdered black people across the state—just like Roof allegedly did on Wednesday evening. (Jenkins 4)

Mississippi continues to debate the issue of the battle emblem on its own state flag: in 2001, the public voted overwhelmingly to *not* remove the emblem—and this past year, in spite of the Charleston massacre, the legislature continues to rebuff proposals to change the flag; the debate has entered the courts with a lawsuit arguing that the flag "is tantamount to hateful government speech" which "encourages or incites private citizens to commit acts of racial violence," even as the Governor has called for another public referendum on the flag. Louisiana is in the midst of a similarly contentious debate in the wake of New Orleans officials' decision to remove four Confederate monuments. The two sides of the issue were summarized by Governor Bentley thus: "I believe in heritage, I believe in history, and I believe we should always honor history, and we do that in Alabama" while at the same time he noted that "we should take into account the sensitivity of all our citizens on all issues" (*New York Times* March 14, 2016, A11). Is the simultaneous honoring of both "history" (including Confederate icons and symbols of racial oppression) and "the sensitivity of all citizens" even possible or desirable? Can we do both—or do we (as Hillary Clinton argued) have to choose?

Such debates are, of course, not only limited to the American South— nor to Ireland and the Irish, the focus of earlier chapters in this study. In the shocking photos that Dylann Roof had posted on his website prior to killing nine people at the Mother Emanuel Church, he was not only waving the Confederate flag as a symbol of his dedication to white supremacy, but he had two other flags stitched to his jacket (see Fig. 6.2): the flags of apartheid-era Rhodesia and South Africa, the banners of racist apartheid in southern Africa and of white supremacist culture. Indeed, most of the photos of Roof that investigators uncovered were from Roof's own website The Last Rhodesian (www.lastrhodesian.com). Rhodesia (now Zimbabwe)

Fig. 6.2 Dylann Roof and other flags

was of course named after Cecil Rhodes, the British tycoon who founded the De Beers diamond empire in South Africa, and later became premier of the then-British colony from 1890 to 1896. In England and America, Rhodes is best remembered as the founder of the Rhodes Scholarships, funded by money he left when he died in 1902, endowing perhaps the most prestigious and coveted postgraduate scholarship in the world; about 8000 scholars from around the world—including former American president Bill Clinton, former New Jersey Senator Bill Bradley, and many others—have studied at Oxford as Rhodes Scholars. But in African history, Rhodes is remembered infamously as an architect of apartheid and racial segregation who believed in the superiority of the Anglo-Saxon race; thus Roof's fascination with the Rhodesian flag. In April 2015, the University of Cape Town in South Africa removed, under pressure from student activists, a statue of Rhodes on its campus. And at Oxford University, the home of the Rhodes Scholarship program, student activists started a campaign called "Rhodes Must Fall," protesting a monument to Rhodes at Oriel College and petitioning for its removal. Just as Rhodes is remembered for both his racist/imperialist ruthlessness and for his generous educational patronage, so also the debate hinges on two separate, incompatible stances. Defenders argue that the past should not be judged by the standards of today, and that to do so would be defacing and erasing history. R.W. Johnson, emeritus fellow of Oxford's Magdalen College, argues that removing the monument is similar to what the Islamic State of Iraq and Syria (ISIS) and Al-Qaeda are currently doing in destroying cultural sites and heritages (like Palmyra) in the Middle East: "I think you have got to respect history." And former Australian Prime Minister Tony Abbott, himself a former Rhodes Scholar, argues that "Oxford would damage its standing as a great university if it were to substitute moral vanity for fair-minded inquiry" (one can hear echoes here of an accusation of "political correctness")—and it should not impose "today's orthodoxies .... on our forebears." In response Brian Kwoba, one of the student protestors and a doctoral candidate at Oxford, notes that Cecil Rhodes had engaged in "stealing land, massacring tens of thousands of black Africans, imposing a regime of unspeakable labor exploitation in the diamond mines and devising pro-apartheid policies." "The significance of taking down the statue is simple," he says: "Cecil Rhodes is the Hitler of southern Africa. Would anyone countenance a statue of Hitler?" In that sense, the Rhodes monument arguably engages in hostile insensitivity to contemporary Oxford students, especially its racial minorities. And the "Rhodes Must Fall" campaign emailed a further response, arguing that "Abbott's comments embody the distortion of the past we are challenging; the monument is not an impartial preservation of history—it is a whitewashed glorification, which erases the histories of millions of black Africans who suffered under colonialism" (*New York Times* December 25, 2015, A12). So which "history" is being distorted or defaced or whitewashed? Indeed, what gets remembered or forgotten, or commemorated or suppressed, is necessarily based not on an unerring and reconstructable historical memory (which does not exist) but on individual versions of historical interpretation—that is, on "writing" history.

How then should we remember and commemorate the past? Is holding on to past grievances simply stoking rancor and preventing unity and harmony (as Renan suggests)? Well, the Mother Emanuel massacre provides clear evidence that nostalgic revisionism and historical amnesia do matter still, and are still very harmful: the Lost Cause worship of icons like the Confederate flag and statues of rebel generals results directly in the rise of the Klan, in the growth of white supremacist hate groups, and in the makeup of Dylann Roof's racist agenda of hatred (which embraced white supremacy and the Third Reich) and his ensuing massacre of black folks. It also continues to contribute to a nostalgia about antebellum Southern culture that encourages a blindness to the realities of both slavery and racial oppression in American history. Witness the comments by even South Carolina's then-Governor, Nikki Haley (now President Trump's Ambassador to the United Nations): a day after she delivered the Republican response to President Obama's 2016 State of the Union Address—in which she also criticized Donald Trump's anti-Muslim and anti-immigrant comments (even as those comments have become a magnet for white supremacist and Klan support of Trump)—Governor Haley explained to reporters: "When you've got immigrants who are coming here legally, we've never in the history of this country passed any laws or done anything based on race or religion." Excuse me? This is a rather startling comment coming out of the mouth of the head of South Carolina, the first state to secede from the Union over the cause of slavery! And even if Governor Haley, herself the daughter of immigrants from India, meant her comment to be taken only in the context of the history of immigration in America, such a comment could still only be made if she was completely ignorant of (or amnesiac about) the history of American immigration. As Leonard Pitts asks:

What about:

The Naturalization Act of 1790, which extended citizenship to "any alien, being a free white person"?

Or the Chinese Exclusion Act of 1882, whose title and intent are self-explanatory?

Or the Immigration Act of 1917, which banned immigrants from East Asia and the Pacific?

Or Ozawa v. U.S., the 1922 Supreme Court decision which declared that Japanese immigrants could not be naturalized?

Or U.S. v. Bhagat Singh Thind, the 1923 high court ruling which said people from India—like Haley's parents—could not become naturalized citizens? (Pitts, "Nikki Haley living in Fantasyland," in *Salt Lake Tribune*, January 17, 2016, O2)

In other words, there are real consequences to such historical amnesia. State education departments are now frequently under pressure from conservative Republican school boards to refrain from teaching any inconvenient truths, as textbooks are scrubbed of ethnic/racial histories that sully the nation's image: as a result, for example, black slaves become recast in American History textbooks as "immigrants and settlers" and as part of the history of American immigration (see http://crfimmigrationed.org/index. php/lessons-for-teachers/71-immigrant-article-1); George Washington's slave is cast as a happy member of the family (even though he successfully runs away); and Southerners under the influence of Lost Cause thinking are convinced that the Civil War had nothing to do with slavery but only with their own sovereignty. Perhaps, contra Renan, it is *not* so good for everyone to learn to forget.

After all, such historical amnesia allows for a willed blindness to actual, continuing social problems and conditions. A Gallup Poll in 1962 found that a startling 85 percent of white Americans said that black children had as good a chance as white children of getting a good education; and a Gallup Poll a year later found almost 50 percent of white Americans believing that black Americans had just as good a chance of getting a job as white Americans—in spite of the fact that, at the same time, 45 percent of whites admitted that they would object if a family member asked a black person home for dinner! This appears not only blind but delusional—in a decade that saw marches for Civil Rights in the South, violent clashes between white Southerners and Civil Rights marches, murders of Civil Rights marchers, the President calling out the National Guard in Alabama and Mississippi to quell segregationist violence, the Watts riots in Los Angeles, and so on. Even in the past few years, two thirds of white Americans still believe that black folks are treated fairly by the police, and about 80 percent of them believe that black children now have the same chance as white children of obtaining a good education. Clearly many of these white Americans are also well-meaning people: as Nicholas Kristof points out, they "look around today, see a black president, and declare problem solved." White Americans' perceptions about race have historically white-washed inconvenient histories and truths, resulting in willful self-deception. Indeed, as Kristof goes on to point out:

> Half of white Americans today say that discrimination against whites is as big a problem as discrimination against blacks. Really? That contradicts overwhelming research showing that blacks are more likely to be suspended from preschool, to be prosecuted for drug use, to receive longer sentences, to be discriminated against in housing, to be denied job interviews, to be rejected by doctors' offices, to suffer bias in almost every measurable sector of daily life. In my mind, an even bigger civil rights outrage in America than abuses by some police officers may be an education system that routinely sends the neediest black students to underfunded, third-rate schools, while directing bountiful resources to affluent white schools.

Kristof suggests that a starting point for white Americans to start waking up from such delusion and amnesia is "to recognize that in practice black lives have not mattered as much as white lives, and that this is an affront to values that we all profess to believe in." (Kristof, "A History of White Delusion," *New York Times* July 14, 2016, A27).

Indeed, our very semantic categories and logic reflect this racial amnesia. At the 2016 Republican Party's National Convention, Florida Governor Rick Scott said that he could remember when "terrorism was something that happened in foreign countries." But how about the four little girls blown to bits in a black church in Birmingham in 1963, or the black NAACP lawyer and his wife (Harry T. and Harriet Moore) killed in 1951 by a bomb in Governor Scott's own state of Florida? (See also Leonard Pitts in *Salt Lake Tribune* July 24, 2016, O2.) In other words, when lone-wolf Muslim individuals kill white people—whether in Orlando or Nice or Munich—we classify these as acts of terrorism (and prosecute them as such under the USA Patriot Act), even if there is no clear evidence that these individuals were actually under the direction of ISIS or Al-Qaeda or the Taliban. But when a 22-year-old white man, Dylann Roof, murders nine black people in a black church in South Carolina while spewing racist hatred of black people—after wearing pro-apartheid, white supremacist flag patches from Rhodesia and South Africa, after proudly photographing himself with a Confederate battle flag, and after saying that he was hoping to ignite a race war—he was *not* charged with terrorism. Professed racist hatred by white people against black people is simply not considered as threatening or dire a phenomenon as professed hatred by brown folks against white folks. No wonder black people in the USA feel a need to remind the nation that "Black Lives Matter."

Ernest Renan's dictum that "it is good for everyone to learn to forget" for the sake of national harmony and unity, and so as not to stoke the embers of old rancors (to let sleeping dogs lie, as it were), can only make sense when the particular rancor or resentment has longed stopped mattering, after a process of reconciliation and national peace: France is no longer fighting the religious medieval wars and no individual French person cares (or even knows) if he or she is a descendant of Huguenots or not, not to speak of an Alan, a Taifale, a Visigoth, and so on. But such is not yet the case in either Northern Ireland or, just as clearly, the USA, where—in spite of advances and the election of a black President, we have not been able to "transcend race"—and where the legacy of the Civil War and of the South's "peculiar institution" has not yet been buried, and where continuing racist attitudes lead to historical nostalgia, distortion, and amnesia that are still very dangerous, violent, and ongoing. One need only think of Dylann Roof.

*   *   *

In the meantime, a possible goal would be to develop something we might call "ethical remembrancing"—a term I am coining, which combines the sort of "ethical remembering" advocated by Paul Ricoeur with the concept of "remembrancing" as the creating of "remembrances" in order to honor the memory of the past (whether a person, thing, battle, and so on). One good place to start—as a case study and example of this larger issue—might be to consider the case of Georgetown University and its black slaves, a case that returns us to the issue of the Irish and slavery in the American South.

In the previous chapter, we looked at how the Irish supported the institution of slavery in the South. This support included Irish priests and Catholic religious orders. Archbishop John Hughes—a native of County

Tyrone in Ireland who emigrated to the United States in 1817, became a priest in 1826, and eventually became the first Archbishop of the Archdiocese of New York—was himself a former overseer of slaves in Maryland; even as a bishop and archbishop, he remained firmly opposed to abolition. Bishop John England had been ordained a priest in 1809 in Cork, Ireland, where he became a close friend and ally of Daniel O'Connell ("The Liberator") in the campaign for Catholic Emancipation. In 1820, England was then sent to South Carolina as the first Catholic Bishop of Charleston—where he soon parted ways with his old friend over O'Connell's criticism of the practice of slavery, instead defending South Carolina and its "brave and generous people." One of Bishop England's protegés, Patrick Neison Lynch, would succeed him as Bishop of Charleston: born in County Fermanagh in Ireland, Lynch is mostly remembered today for his vocal support of both slavery and the Confederacy; as a result, he was named in 1864 by President Jefferson Davis to be the Confederate's delegate to the Vatican to argue for the Confederate cause, for which he composed an extended pro-slavery treatise. Bishop Lynch, who also was in charge of the management of the slaves owned by the Catholic diocese, owned 95 slaves himself.

Indeed, the pattern for Irish Catholic acceptance of slavery had been set earlier by Bishop John Carroll, of the famed Irish Catholic Carroll family in Maryland; he became the first Catholic bishop and later the first archbishop in the United States, overseeing the Archdiocese of Baltimore, Maryland; he also founded Georgetown College (now Georgetown University), the oldest Catholic university in the United States. Carroll's Irish-born father had married into a plantation-owning family, and so John grew up on a large, slave-owning plantation in what is now Prince George's County in Maryland. The colonial Province of Maryland had been founded as a Catholic haven, even though the colony was primarily Protestant; the Catholic population gradually moved out of the public eye and onto private manors and plantations, safe havens for free practice of their faith—including a number of plantations, run with slave labor, owned by the Jesuit missions. The Carroll family were prominent leaders in Maryland and in the original Colonies (Gilbert Stuart painted a portrait of Bishop Carroll): his cousin Charles Carroll was one of the Founding Fathers and a signer of the Declaration of Independence (1776) in Philadelphia; John's older brother Daniel was one of only five men to sign both the Articles of Confederation and Perpetual Union (1778) and the US Constitution (1787). John himself (who had become a Jesuit priest in

1753) was sent by the Continental Congress in 1776—along with Benjamin Franklin, Samuel Chase, and his cousin Charles—on a mission to Quebec in an attempt to persuade French Canada to join the Revolution against England.

After the war, Carroll and five other Jesuit priests met at Whitemarsh, Maryland in June 1783 to start discussing how to maintain their properties and carry on their missionary work; they gradually laid out a foundation for the Catholic Church in this country. In 1784 Pope Pius VI appointed Carroll as the "Superior of the Missions in the thirteen United States of North America." A year after that, in a letter to Rome, Carroll reported on the status of Catholics in Maryland, stating that they included 9000 freemen, 3000 children, and "3000 negro slaves" (O'Donovan 2). Carroll himself owned more than 100 slaves.

In 1791, Bishop Carroll (he was now the Bishop of the Archdiocese of Baltimore, and would become Archbishop in 1808) founded Georgetown College, entrusting the administration of the school to the Jesuits. Thus Georgetown was, from the start, both a Jesuit and a strongly Irish institution. Through the early decades of the nineteenth century, Georgetown's operational expenses were funded in large part from the profits of the Jesuit plantations in Maryland (whose slaves were often donated by wealthy parishioners). The Maryland Jesuits had built their provincial enterprise on 12,000 acres of plantations scattered across Maryland. But by mid-century, these plantations were floundering: "[A]lthough the Jesuits owned hundreds of slaves, land was costly to maintain and the Jesuits were more concerned with upholding their priestly duties than running plantations" (Monyak 4); as a result of the failing plantations, the College kept accruing debt and the Jesuit administrators felt increasing pressures to free themselves of the plantations.

It was at this point that yet another Irish American Jesuit priest, Father Thomas Mulledy—"a quick-witted and quick-tempered son of Irish immigrants" (Quallen, "Slavery" 2)—would, at the young age of 35, become President of Georgetown College in 1829. In 1838 Father Mulledy also became the provincial (head) of the Maryland Society of Jesus, and he—along with Father William McSherry, his successor as Georgetown president—engineered the sale of 272 slaves owned by the Maryland Jesuits. As Matthew Quallen writes: "What ensued marks the most shameful chapter in the Georgetown Jesuits' long history. Families were divided as people were forced onto ships. Slaves as young as 9 months and as old as 75 were corralled and uprooted. Many slaves panicked. Several fled into the surrounding woods" (Quallen, "Georgetown" 2). As the *New York Times* (April 17, 2016) notes: "The enslaved were grandmothers and grandfathers, carpenters and blacksmiths, pregnant women and anxious fathers, children and infants, who were fearful, bewildered and despairing as they saw their families and communities ripped apart by the sale of 1838." The slaves—their families split apart—were shipped off to plantations in Louisiana, where they were treated brutally (in contrast to their relatively more humane treatment in Maryland) and where they, as Catholic converts, were not allowed to practice their Catholic faith. As Suzanne Monyak writes: "After nearly 200 years, the Society's plantations had finally been disbanded; the 1838 slave sale marked the end of Jesuit-run plantations in Maryland" (Monyak 5). But the sale—netting what would today be about 3.3 million dollars—did successfully pay off Georgetown's debts and was crucial in the continuation of the institution now known as Georgetown University.

But the sale also darkened Mulledy's reputation, as many of his fellow Jesuits were outraged. As *The New York Times* reported (April 17, 2016, A16): "Father Mulledy promised his superiors that the slaves would continue to practice their religion. Families would not be separated. And the money raised by the sale would not be used to pay off debt or for operating expenses. None of those conditions were met." One Dutch Jesuit, Father Peter Havermans, S.J., protested: "No one does this sort of thing except evil persons, such as slave traders who care about nothing but money .... I tell you this will be a tragic and disgraceful affair" (Monyak 5). The priests worried that the new plantations would not allow their black converts to practice their faith and go to Mass on Sunday, that families would be separated, and that the conditions in the plantations in Louisiana were known to be particularly brutal. The response from fellow Jesuits was such that the next year Mulledy was asked to resign from his position as provincial—and in the ensuing uproar, he was called to Rome and reassigned (though he would eventually return and, years later, serve a second term as Georgetown president). The following year, Pope Gregory XVI ordered Catholics to stop engaging in "this traffic in Blacks ... no matter what pretext or excuse" (*New York Times* April 17, 2016, A16). Commenting on his humiliation and disgrace, Mulledy acknowledged that "no doubt I deserve it" (Quallen, "Georgetown" 2).

* * *

Georgetown University is, today, one of the nation's elite universities, with more than 17,500 students and an endowment of 1.5 billion dollars. It is also a diverse urban campus in the midst of the cosmopolitan nation's capital, a university with a significant African American student body in a city with an extremely large African American population. So it is easy now to forget that this well-known educational institution was, to a great extent, built by black slaves. In January 2015, an essay by staff writer Suzanne Monyak, published in *The Hoya*, the University newspaper, reminded the Georgetown community of that history. Her story's title minced no words: "Built by Slaves and Jesuits: Georgetown's past is mired in the institution of slavery." This startling spotlight on Georgetown's hidden past was followed by a process of communal soul-searching by the University community, not only students and faculty/staff but also its alumni (more on that later). Then on Sunday April 17, 2016, the *New York Times* published a long, front-page story (by Rachel L. Swarns) on this process, titled "Georgetown Confronts Its Role in Nation's Slave Trade"—thus bringing this Georgetown history, as well as the ensuing questions of how to remember/commemorate and how to make reparations, to the awareness of the general public outside the University. The story's subheading was revealing: "What Does the University Owe Descendants of 272 Slaves?" In other words, how can one ethically and thoughtfully remember and try to repair—as much as one can at this point—such a tragic and disgraceful episode in the institution's past?

The *Times* article was detailed, insightful, thoughtful, and powerful—and fed an already ongoing national self-examination (during the same spring as the Freddie Gray incident in Baltimore, the "Black Lives Matter" movement, and so on) about how to come to terms with the history and legacy of racism against black people in this country. But not mentioned in the *Times* story was another, somewhat tangential, not very well-known, but certainly not irrelevant story—involving yet another Irish American Catholic priest. For the Jesuit priests at Georgetown in the nineteenth-century had been, as I already mentioned, outraged and fully aware of the tragedy perpetrated by Fathers Mulledy and McSherry in 1838. What follows here is the story of the Reverend Patrick Healy, S.J.

Patrick Francis Healy (see Fig. 6.3) was born in 1834 in Macon, Georgia, to an Irish American plantation owner, Michael Healy, and his mulatto slave, Mary Eliza, with whom Michael Healy had fallen in love (and went on to live with for the rest of his life). By law, then, Patrick Healy was himself a slave, having been born into slavery. However, he

Fig. 6.3 Patrick
Francis Healy, S.J.

inherited fair skin and Irish features from his father's side, and so was able oftentimes to pass as a white person. Nevertheless, as a slave under the nation's "one-drop rule" (the accepted principle that even "one drop" of black blood—whatever that meant—made you black), he had no chance of rising up the economic or social class ladders in Southern white society; indeed, educating slaves was illegal in the State of Georgia. But his father sent the Healy children north to be raised and educated as Irish Americans. Patrick (and his brothers) would go on to attend a newly founded Jesuit college, The College of Holy Cross in Worcester, Massachusetts. After graduation, Patrick entered the Jesuit order as a novitiate, and was sent by the order to Europe to continue his education at the Catholic University of Leuven in Belgium, where he earned a doctorate. In 1864 he was ordained into the priesthood. Upon his return to the United States in 1866, he was hired by Georgetown as a faculty member, in time rising to become Prefect of Studies (i.e., academic dean). So: if Patrick Healy was not allowed to successfully navigate the world of white Southern culture, having been born into slavery, was he then able to "pass" (as an Irish American) in the less restrictive culture and order of Jesuit priests?

In fact, though, the story is more complicated than that: for historical sources make clear that the Jesuits at Georgetown were quite aware of Healy's mixed-race identity and background—and clearly decided to keep his African ancestry and slave roots hidden from the rest of the Georgetown community. This was mid-century Washington, DC, and the Georgetown student body before the War was largely made up of white Southerners (many of whom would go on to fight for the Confederacy), and was again full of white Southerners after the War; both the town of Georgetown and the University campus had a distinctively Southern atmosphere. The Jesuit administration of the University knew what would happen to Healy's life and career if it were known that the Prefect of Studies was actually a black slave. Think of what this means: these Catholic, predominantly Irish, priests were willing—in defiance of the prevailing pro-slavery bent in the Irish American community—to reject racial discrimination among their own ranks, and to show (if only to themselves) that the outrages perpetrated by Father Mulledy a couple of decades earlier on the order's 272 black, Catholic slaves was not consistent with their own Christian beliefs and values. I would suggest that the process of reparation and reconciliation had begun even then, albeit in secret.

Indeed, the story did not end there. In May 1873, the University president at the time, Father John Early, S.J., died suddenly. And the University's Board of Directors decided to name Patrick Healy, still only 39-years-old, to take over as the 29th President of Georgetown University. Father Healy proved to be a game-changer for Georgetown: as Monyak notes: "Under his presidency, Georgetown pushed for modernization and evolved from a small college into a national university, prompting some to refer to him as the university's second founder" (Monyak 7). Influenced by his education in Europe, he modernized the Georgetown curriculum by requiring courses in the sciences; he expanded and upgraded the law school and the medical school. And he oversaw the construction (1877–1891) of the University's flagship building, now named Healy Hall in his honor (also now listed as a National Historic Landmark), literally cementing his legacy as the most important President of Georgetown University.

Notably, it would not be until the 1960s, during the Civil Rights movement, that Father Healy's actual background and racial identity became public knowledge. Thus, in retrospect, he has now been recognized not only as a powerful shaper of a leading American institution of higher learning—but as the very first African American to earn a PhD, the first African

American to become a Jesuit priest, and the first one to serve as a president of a predominantly white college! These achievements form a legacy made secretly possible by the Jesuit priests at Georgetown in the nineteenth century, and in themselves constitute a notable part of the school's historical relationship, and its attempts to come to terms, with slavery.

On August 24, 2015, in the wake of the revelations earlier that year which had brought to light Georgetown's slave-owning past and the outrage of 1838, University President John J. DeGioia (the first lay President of the school) sent out to the University community "A Message Regarding Mulledy Hall" (which was being renovated). In his message, DeGioia adds:

> This is also an occasion for reflection and deep contemplation about the history of our University, including those moments in our history that are challenging, complex, and that run counter to the values that we seek to uphold. The opening of this new residential community—located in these historic buildings on our campus [including Mulledy Hall]—calls our attention to a very difficult history, our own institution's historical ties to slavery. ("Message" 1)

Rehearsing the history of Father Mulledy's sale of the 272 slaves owned by the Society of Jesus in Maryland, DeGioia notes that "[Mulledy]'s actions represent a difficult past that is contrary to the values and mission of our University .... As we re-open the Mulledy building, we take this opportunity to again look directly at the historical moment of which he was a part and the role that our University played in the institution of slavery." Noting that they were now (two months after the Mother Emanuel massacre) living at a moment in the nation's history "marked by moments of tragedy and violence fueled by racism and prejudice," DeGioia writes that he will officially launch a campaign to reflect on this past and that "in the coming weeks, I will appoint a steering committee comprised of faculty, students, alumni, staff and administrators" so that, as a community, Georgetown can reflect on and "confront difficult events" and "learn from one another" so as "to determine how we may best move forward toward justice and truth." Indeed, a month later, on September 24, DeGioia announced the formation of the "Working Group on Slavery, Memory, and Reconciliation."

As the *New York Times* cover story on Sunday April 17, 2016 noted about this "Working Group": "Now, with racial protests roiling college campuses, an unusual collection of Georgetown professors, students, alumni and genealogists is trying to find out what happened to those 272 men, women and children. And they are confronting a particularly wrenching question: What, if anything, is owed to the descendants of slaves who were sold to help ensure the college's survival?" (A1) To begin with, in November the University decided (spurred by both student protests and the Working Group) to remove the names of Father Mulledy and Father McSherry, the two University presidents who had been involved in the sale of the slaves, from the names of the two campus buildings already named after them. But one alumnus, following the protests and proceedings from a distance, felt that this wasn't enough: Richard J. Cellini, the chief executive of a technology company in Cambridge, Massachusetts, a practicing Catholic and a white man, felt troubled that nothing had been done to find out what happened to those slaves nor to compensate their descendants: "This is not a disembodied group of people who are nameless and faceless .... These are real people with real names and real descendants." So Mr. Cellini set up a nonprofit organization titled the Georgetown Memory Project, hiring eight genealogists from among fellow alumni to research the matter alongside Dr. Adam Rothman, a historian at Georgetown and a member of the Working Group.

Using archival records, the genealogists uncovered a story of Jesuit priests who had converted their slaves and required them to attend Mass, some of whom had tried to run away under harsh plantation conditions, as well as anguished protests by some of the priests over their role in this system of plantation slavery. The records showed that the slaves were sent, in several different ships, from the Maryland plantations to the docks of New Orleans, and from there most of them ended up in three different plantations near Baton Rouge. They learned that the slaves' new owners had indeed broken their promises, for most of them were sent to plantations far from any Catholic churches and priests, as reported by Father James Van de Velde, a Jesuit who visited Louisiana in 1848; Father Van de Velde wrote to Father Mulledy, now in his second term as president of Georgetown, pleading for money to build a church so as to "provide for the salvation of those poor people, who are now utterly neglected"; as the *Times* articles notes, "there is no indication that he received any response."

The hope of the Georgetown Memory Group genealogists was to start identifying and finding the descendants of these slaves. Records showed priests at the Jesuit plantations recounting panic, fear, and attempted escapes as their slaves were put into the several vessels headed to New Orleans. One of these was a 13-year-old boy named Cornelius Hawkins, who was put onboard the "Katharine Jackson." But black folks in the nineteenth century—enslaved, discriminated against, and often unable to read and write—tended to leave very few historical traces and records. So Cornelius Hawkins's name doesn't resurface again till 1851, on a cotton plantation near Maringouin, Louisiana; and in 1870 his name is listed in the census for the first time, as a 48-year-old father and husband, now a farmer and a freeman. As Rachel Swarns writes: "He might have disappeared from view again for a time, save for something few could have counted on: his deep, abiding faith. It was his Catholicism, born on the Jesuit plantations of his childhood, that would provide researchers with a road map to his descendants" (A16). Since Hawkins's descendants had also embraced the Catholic faith, Judy Riffel, one of the genealogists, was able to follow a trail of church baptisms, weddings, and burials—and these church records eventually led her to Baton Rouge, to a woman named Maxine Crump. Maxine Crump is a familiar face in Baton Rouge: she had been the city's first black woman TV news anchor, and now, at 69, still runs a nonprofit organization teaching ways to combat institutional racism. Ms. Crump was stunned when she was contacted—for the whole story was completely new to her—except for the name Cornelius, or "Neely" as Hawkins had been known: for "the name [Neely] had been passed down from generation to generation in her family. Her great-uncle had the name, as did one of her cousins. Now, for the first time, Ms. Crump understood its origins" (A16). Exclaiming "Oh my god, oh my God," Ms. Crump began to realize that "Now they [my ancestors] are real to me." When Ms. Riffel, the genealogist, met Ms. Crump in Baton Rouge and told her that she thought she knew where Cornelius might be buried, Ms. Crump knew right away where to go, too: for there was only one Catholic cemetery in Maringouin. Once there, the two women found an old, toppled gravestone that clearly still reads: "Neely Hawkins. Died April 16, 1902." (A16).

*   *   *

Mr. Cellini's genealogists have to date traced more than 200 of the 272 slaves from Maryland to Louisiana and elsewhere, and have started contacting a few of the possibly thousands of descendants still living. The *Times* reports further: "Meanwhile, Georgetown's working group has been weighing whether the university should apologize for profiting from slave labor, create a memorial to those enslaved and provide scholarships for their descendants, among other possibilities" (A16). Says Adam Rothman, the historian in the group: "It's hard to know what could possibly reconcile a story like this. What can you do to make amends?" Maxine Crump, for one, says she doesn't believe in "casual institutional apologies" but would prefer to see a scholarship program to help descendants attend Georgetown University.

How can one make amends? And how should we remember and commemorate? What can we be allowed to forget? These are the questions that this entire study has been steeped in—and are the same ones now confronting Georgetown's Working Group. Other universities—including Harvard, Brown, Columbia, and the University of Virginia—are also having to grapple with the legacy of the past, as recent student protests have focused on their institutional histories steeped in the slave trade. Drew Gilpin Faust, Harvard University's current president, admitted in March 2016 that the University has been "directly complicit in America's system of racial bondage" and proceeded to commemorate four slaves who had worked in the households of early Harvard administrators. In April 2016, almost 20 colleges and universities (including Virginia, William and Mary, and Roanoke) participated in a conference to discuss efforts to study and memorialize the black slaves that had built and served these schools. And Harvard's Faust began planning to host a national conference in 2017 on the topic of universities and slavery. As the *New York Times* reported (November 7, 2016, A11), the responses have been mixed: "Some applaud efforts to bring a largely untold history to light. Others argue that the focus on the past exacerbates racial tensions on campuses and distracts from more pressing matters." Here we have a specific iteration of Renan's question: is it not better for everyone to learn to forget, so as not to exacerbate the animosities of the past in an effort to maintain the unity and harmony of the present?

For his part, Georgetown's President DeGioia is "Intent on Reckoning With Georgetown's Slavery-Stained Past" (as the *New York Times* titled its follow-up story on July 11, 2016)—and has been confronting and pursuing these questions head-on. As his Working Group continues to debate whether Georgetown should apologize, or should create a memorial to the slaves, or should offer scholarships to their descendants, or all the above (they are planning to release their report in summer 2016), DeGioia has traveled to speak to slave descendants in Spokane (WA), New Orleans, and Baton Rouge. And he has met with alumni, some of whom are troubled by DeGioia's support of the student protesters' and the Working Group's demands to rename Mulledy Hall and McSherry Hall, arguing that "by focusing on the wrongs of the 19th century, Mr. DeGioia is unnecessarily besmirching the reputation of a venerable institution" (A11). Again, we face the questions: how much do we need to remember, how much can we be allowed to forget, and how much perhaps do we need forget in order for there to be unity, peace, and reconciliation? Or as DeGioia himself put it, acknowledging the worries of his doubters: "Why is there a need to resurface the pain and the agony of this part of history? Haven't we moved beyond this?" But he also pointed out that both the recent series of police shootings of black men, and the persistent economic disparity between the races, suggest that we, as a culture, have not been able to sufficiently and collectively come to terms with the legacy of slavery, and with the institutionalized racism that it entailed and condoned: "I don't think we can say we've sufficiently moved beyond it."

And so in June 2016, President DeGioia flew to Louisiana and drove a rental car to Maringouin, where—alongside Maxine Crump—he visited the sugar cane and cotton fields where Georgetown's slaves, including Neely Hawkins, had once worked, and visited the cemetery where Neely and other descendants were buried. And he met with dozens of the descendants whom Mr. Cellini's genealogists have now been able to find, answering their questions—as well as the stated skepticism, and understandable anger, from some of them—about the issues of remembrancing, reparations, and reconciliation. DeGioia acknowledged that he was just starting the process of talking with descendants and their families, and of trying to address their concerns: "He told the descendants that he hoped Georgetown could help reknit families torn apart by the sale, providing them with access to records about the Jesuit slaves in the university archives and possibly hosting a gathering of descendants on campus" (A11). This might not have satisfied everyone—but it was at least a start. And at least he was there.[2]

NOTES

1. As Jenkins goes on to argue: "But if Roof's senseless rampage tells us anything, it's that while the Confederate flag is certainly about heritage, it *is and has always been* about hate. By being part of Roof's constellation of negative influences, the symbol of the Confederacy—and the history behind it—is once again associated with the pointless murder of people of color."
2. On September 1, 2016, the Working Group released its 102-page report, and President DeGioia announced—to an audience of hundreds of students, faculty members, alumni, and descendants—that the University will

start to put in place a series of measures to atone for its past, based on the Working Group's recommendations. These include: a formal apology; awarding preferential status in the admissions process to the descendants of the 272 slaves; the creation of an institute for the study of slavery; and a public memorial to the slaves who helped build and fund Georgetown (the Working Group's report suggested that black slaves had worked not only on the Jesuit plantations but in constructing the school buildings and toiling on campus). The Group's report had also raised the possibility of offering scholarships to the descendants, but this was not yet part of the announced measures. Nevertheless, historians noted that the decision to offer preferential treatment in admissions—similar to the "legacy" preferences for descendants of alumni—was an unprecedented move by a university. Furthermore, DeGioia announced that Mulledy Hall and McSherry Hall would now be renamed Isaac Hall and Anne Marie Becraft Hall—to commemorate one of the slaves (Isaac Hawkins, Cornelius Hawkins's grandfather) shipped to Louisiana in 1838 and a nineteenth-century black educator (Anne Marie Becraft) who founded a school in Washington, DC for black girls. As President DeGioia explained:

> This community participated in the institution of slavery. This original evil that shaped the early years of the Republic was present here. We have been able to hide from this truth, bury this truth, ignore and deny this truth.
>
> As a community and as individuals, we cannot do our best work if we refuse to take ownership of such a critical part of our history. We must acknowledge it. (*New York Times* September 2, 2016, A1, A14; *Salt Lake Tribune* September 2, 2016, A6)

WORKS CITED

DeGioia, John J. "A Message Regarding Mulledy Hall." August 24, 2015. https://president.georgetown.edu/mulledy-hall

Hemmer, Nicole. "Those Two Other Flags." *US News* June 23, 2015. https://www.usnews.com/opinion/blogs/nicole-hemmer/2015/06/23/confederate-flag-wasnt-the-only-inspiration-for-dylann-storm-roof?int=opinion-rec

Horwitz, Tony. *Confederates in the Attic: Dispatches from the Unfinished Civil War*. New York: Vintage, 1999.

Janney, Caroline E. "The Lost Cause." *Encyclopedia Virginia*. Ed. Brendan Wolfe. 8 Jan. 2013. Virginia Foundation for the Humanities. 9 May 2011: http://www.EncyclopediaVirginia.org/Lost_Cause_The

Jenkins, Jack. "How the Charleston Shooting is Linked to the Confederate Flag, According to a South Carolinian." *ThinkProgress* June 19, 2015. https://thinkprogress.org/how-the-charleston-shooting-is-linked-to-the-confederate-flag-according-to-a-south-carolinian-1b97034fb56f

Monyak, Suzanne. "Built by Slaves and Jesuits: Georgetown's past is mired in the institution of slavery." *The Hoya* January 30, 2015. http://www.thehoya.com/slavery/

O'Donovan, Louis. "John Carroll." *The Catholic Encyclopedia*. Vol. 3. New York: Robert Appleton Company, 1908. 28 Jul. 2016. http://www.newadvent.org/cathen/03381b.htm

Quallen, Matthew. "Georgetown, Financed by Slave Trading." *The Hoya* September 26, 2014. http://www.thehoya.com/georgetown-financed-by-slave-trading/

_____. "Slavery Inextricably Tied to Georgetown's Growth." *The Hoya* October 23, 2015. http://ww.thehoya.com/quallen-slavery-inextricably-tied-to-georgetowns-growth/

Renan, Ernest. "What Is a Nation?" Trans. Martin Thom. In Homi K. Bhabha, ed., *Nation and Narration*. 8–22.

Ricoeur, Paul. *Memory, History, Forgetting*. Trans. Kathleen Blamey and David Pellauer. Chicago: University of Chicago Press, 2004.

Yerushalmi, Yosef Hayim. *Zakhor: Jewish History and Jewish Memory*. New York: Schocken Books, 1989.

CHAPTER 7

Afterword

The chapters in this book have presented a series of cases studies, in Irish history and in American history, having to do with the processes of remembering, narrating, commemorating, and, indeed, forgetting, the past—by exploring the relationships between history and literature, between memory and writing/fiction, between forgetting and falsification. If, as I suggested in the opening chapter, all memory and all history are versions of narrative, of interpretation, of writing fiction, of desire—and if, indeed, there is a need both to remember and to forget, then how can we decide what we should remember and what we should forget?

In addressing these questions, this study has explored the advantages and the needs, as well as the ethical complexities and the very real dangers, of forgetting. Whereas both Yerushalmi and Kundera have, in their writing, taken strong stances on the dangers of forgetting, Joyce's texts, as I have shown, point out the dangers of *both* forgetting and remembering—for, in Joyce's works, even "remembering" is a kind of forgetting, a distortion and covering-up of brutal realities and facts which gloss over the complex realities of the Irish people and their history. In the end, after this series of striking case studies, I have, very intentionally, resisted trying to write a "conclusion" to this study—settling instead for this brief Afterword: for I do not want to make any overarching or reductive argument about the very complex nuances and valences surrounding both memory and forgetting, as explored in these chapters. I especially refuse to trumpet the notion

© The Author(s) 2018   149
V. J. Cheng, *Amnesia and the Nation*, New Directions in Irish and Irish
American Literature, https://doi.org/10.1007/978-3-319-71818-7_7

that all history and memory (and facts) are nothing more than versions of writing fiction—because, even though that may be true in an absolute and theoretical sense, I wish to dispute the notion that therefore all memory-work—which is to say, that the narratives of history, both personal and collective—are all thus equivalent, are all the same, simply because (after all) they are all fictions. And so I decided to end the book with a case study of "ethical remembrancing" precisely to distance this study from such a dangerous notion—and to underscore the point that there are important ethical choices and nuances involved in how we remember and how we forget. Such nuances and complexities are especially and urgently important, at this moment (Spring 2017) in which I am writing these sentences, in our contemporary, post-Trump world—one which blithely substitutes "alternative facts" for any inconvenient truths, and which willfully distorts facts and history to fit one's own purposes. In a world in which everything from the Tiananmen Massacre to legitimate elections results can be expunged, manipulated, or hacked away from history, and in which President Trump's daily comments repeatedly distort reality and manufacture "truths" by openly lying, we need to be ever more vigilant that manipulative and self-serving distortions involved in both remembering and forgetting cannot be tolerated, and will be recognized as the willful creation of very dangerous fictions.

WORKS CITED

Anderson, Benedict. *Imagined Communities: Reflections on the Origin and Spread of Nationalism*. Revised edition. London: Verso, 1991.

Arnold, Matthew. "On the Study of Celtic Literature." 1910. *English Literature and Irish Politics*, vol. 9 of *The Complete Prose Works of Matthew Arnold*. Ed. R. H. Super. Ann Arbor: University of Michigan Press, 1973.

Bender, Abby. *Israelites in Erin: Exodus, Revolution, and the Irish Revival*. Syracuse, NY: Syracuse University Press, 2015.

Bhabha, Homi K. "DissemiNation: Time, Narrative, and the Margins of the Modern Nation." In *Nation and Narration*, ed. Homi K. Bhabha. London: Routledge, 1990. 291–322.

————, ed. *Nation and Narration*. London: Routledge, 1990.

Cairns, David, and Shaun Richards. *Writing Ireland: Colonialism, Nationalism, and Culture*. Manchester: Manchester University Press, 1988.

Casey, Edward S. *Remembering: A Phenomenological Study*. Second Edition. Bloomington: Indiana University Press, 2000.

Cheng, Vincent J. *Shakespeare and Joyce: A Study of "Finnegans Wake."* University Park: Penn State University Press, 1984.

————. *Joyce, Race, and Empire*. Cambridge: Cambridge University Press, 1995.

————. *Inauthentic: The Anxiety Over Culture and Identity*. New Brunswick, NJ: Rutgers University Press, 2004.

————. "Nationalism, Celticism, and Cosmopolitanism in *A Portrait*." In *A Portrait of the Artist as a Young Man: Case Studies in Contemporary Criticism*, Second Edition. Ed. R. Brandon Kershner. Boston: Bedford/St. Martin's, 2006. 389–412.

© The Author(s) 2018
151
V. J. Cheng, *Amnesia and the Nation*, New Directions in Irish and Irish American Literature, https://doi.org/10.1007/978-3-319-71818-7

————. "A Chronology of *The Good Soldier.*" In Ford, Ford Madox, *The Good Soldier.* Ed. Martin Stannard. New York: Norton Critical Edition, 2012. 391–395.

Connerton, Paul. *How Modernity Forgets.* Cambridge: Cambridge University Press, 2009.

Deane, Seamus. "National Character and National Audience: Races, Crowds, and Readers." In *Critical Approaches to Anglo-Irish Literature,* eds. Michael Allen and Angela Wilcox. Totowa, NJ: Barnes & Noble, 1989. 40–52.

DeGioia, John J. "A Message Regarding Mulledy Hall." August 24, 2015. https://president.georgetown.edu/mulledy-hall

Duffy, Enda. *The Subaltern Ulysses.* Minneapolis: University of Minnesota Press, 1994.

Duffy, Sean. *The Illustrated History of Ireland.* London: McGraw-Hill, 2002.

Eagleton, Terry. "Form and Ideology in the Anglo-Irish Novel." *Bullan* 1.1 (1994): 17–26.

Ellmann, Richard. *James Joyce.* Revised edition. Oxford: Oxford University Press, 1982.

Encyclopaedia Britannica: The New Encyclopaedia Britannica, fifteenth edition, *Micropaedia* vol. 2 (page 448: "Boyne, Battle of the"). Chicago: Encyclopaedia Britannica Inc., 1992.

Faulkner, William. *Requiem for a Nun.* New York: Vintage, 1951.

Fitzgerald, F. Scott. *The Great Gatsby.* New York: Scribner, 1925, 2004.

Ford, Ford Madox. *The Good Soldier: A Tale of Passion.* New York: Vintage International, 1989.

Foster, R. F. *Modern Ireland 1600–1972.* London: Penguin, 1988.

————, ed. *The Oxford Illustrated History of Ireland.* Oxford: Oxford University Press, 1989.

Frow, John. *Time and Commodity Culture: Essays in Cultural Theory and Postmodernity.* Oxford: Clarendon Press, 1997.

————. From "'*Toute la memoire du monde:* Repetition and Forgetting.'" In Rossington and Whitehead 150–156.

Gao, Helen. "Forgetting Tiananmen." *New York Times,* June 4, 2014, page A21.

Gibbons, Luke. *Transformations in Irish Culture.* Cork: Cork Univ. Press, 1996.

————. "'Where Wolfe Tone's statue was not': Joyce, monuments and memory." In McBride 139–59.

Gifford, Don, and Robert J. Seidman. *"Ulysses" Annotated: Notes for James Joyce's "Ulysses."* Revised edition. Berkeley: University of California Press, 1988.

Glasheen, Adaline. *Third Census of "Finnegans Wake."* Berkeley: Univ. of California Press, 1977.

Gleeson, David T. *The Irish in the South, 1815–1877.* Chapel Hill: University of North Carolina Press, 2001.

————. "Another 'Lost Cause': The Irish in the South Remember the Confederacy." *Southern Cultures* 17.1 (Spring 2011: *The Irish*): 50–74.

Goodby, John, et al. *Irish Studies: The Essential Glossary*. London: Arnold, 2003.

Hayden, Tom, ed. *Irish Hunger: Personal Reflections on the Legacy of the Famine*. Boulder: Roberts Rinehart; Dublin: Wolfhound Press, 1997.

Hemmer, Nicole. "Those Two Other Flags." *US News* June 23, 2015. https://www.usnews.com/opinion/blogs/nicole-hemmer/2015/06/23/confederate-flag-wasnt-the-only-inspiration-for-dylann-storm-roof?int=opinion-rec

Higgins, Geraldine. "Tara, the O'Haras, and the Irish *Gone with the Wind*." *Southern Cultures* 17.1 (Spring 2011: *The Irish*): 30–49.

Horwitz, Tony. *Confederates in the Attic: Dispatches from the Unfinished Civil War*. New York: Vintage, 1999.

Hyde, Douglas. "The Necessity for De-Anglicising Ireland." 1892. *Language, Lore and Lyrics, Essays and Lectures*. By Hyde. Ed. Breandan O Conaire. Dublin: Irish Academic Press, 1986.

Ignatiev, Noel. *How the Irish Became White*. New York: Routledge, 1995.

Janney, Caroline E. "The Lost Cause." *Encyclopedia Virginia*. Ed. Brendan Wolfe. 8 Jan. 2013. Virginia Foundation for the Humanities. 9 May 2011: http://www.EncyclopediaVirginia.org/Lost_Cause_The

Jenkins, Jack. "How the Charleston Shooting is Linked to the Confederate Flag, According to a South Carolinian." *ThinkProgress* June 19, 2015. https://thinkprogress.org/how-the-charleston-shooting-is-linked-to-the-confederate-flag-according-to-a-south-carolinian-1b97034fb56f

Joyce, James. *Dubliners: Text, Criticism, and Notes*, eds. Robert Scholes and A. Walton Litz. New York: Viking, 1969.

———. *A Portrait of the Artist as a Young Man: Text, Criticism, and Notes*, ed. Chester G. Anderson. New York: Viking, 1968.

———. *Ulysses*. Eds. Hans Walter Gabler et al. New York: Vintage, 1986.

———. *Finnegans Wake*. New York: Viking, 1939.

———. *Stephen Hero*. Eds. John J. Slocum and Herbert Cahoon. New York: New Directions, 1959.

———. *The Critical Writings of James Joyce*. Eds. Ellsworth Mason and Richard Ellmann. New York: Viking, 1959.

———. *Letters of James Joyce*, II and III. Ed. Richard Ellmann. New York: Viking, 1966.

Kee, Robert. *The Green Flag: A History of Irish Nationalism*. London: Weidenfeld and Nicolson, 1972.

———. *Ireland: A History*. Boston: Little, Brown, 1982.

Kenner, Hugh. *Ulysses*. Baltimore, MD: Johns Hopkins University Press, 1987.

Kiberd, Declan. *Inventing Ireland: The Literature of the Modern Nation*. Cambridge, MA: Harvard University Press, 1995.

———. "The Periphery and the Center." In Waters 5–22.

Kundera, Milan. *The Book of Laughter and Forgetting*. Trans. Michael Henry Heim. New York: Penguin, 1981.

———. *The Unbearable Lightness of Being*. Trans. Michael Henry Heim. New York: Harper & Row, 1985.

Leerssen, Joep. "Monument and trauma: varieties of remembrance." In McBride, 204–222.

Lenihan, Padraig. *1690: Battle of the Boyne*. Tempus, 2005.

Lethem, Jonathan. *The Vintage Book of Amnesia*. New York: Random House, 2000.

Lloyd, David. "Writing in the Shit: Beckett, Nationalism, and the Colonial Subject." *Modern Fiction Studies* 35.1 (Spring 1989): 71–86.

Lukacher, Ned. *Primal Scenes: Literature, Philosophy, Psychoanalysis*. Ithaca, NY: Cornell University Press, 1986.

Luria, A. R. *The Mind of a Mnemonist: A Little Book about a Vast Memory*. New York: Basic Books, 1968.

———. *The Man with a Shattered World: The History of a Brain Wound*. Cambridge, MA: Harvard University Press, 1972.

Marx, Karl. From *The Eighteenth Brumaire of Louis Bonaparte*. In Rossington and Whitehead 97–101.

McBride, Ian, ed. *History and Memory in Modern Ireland*. Cambridge: Cambridge Univ. Press, 2001.

———. "Introduction: memory and national identity in modern Ireland." Introduction to McBride, ed., *History and Memory in Modern Ireland*, 1–42.

McHugh, Roland. *Annotations to "Finnegans Wake."* Baltimore: Johns Hopkins Univ. Press, 1980.

Moore, Thomas. *Moore's Irish Melodies: The Illustrated 1846 Edition*. Mineola, NY: Dover Publications, 2000.

Monyak, Suzanne. "Built by Slaves and Jesuits: Georgetown's past is mired in the institution of slavery." *The Hoya* January 30, 2015. http://www.thehoya. com/slavery/

Nietzsche, Friedrich. *From* "On the Uses and Disadvantages of History for Life." In Rossington and Whitehead 102–108.

Nolan, Emer. *James Joyce and Nationalism*. London: Routledge, 1995.

Nora, Pierre. *Les lieux de mémoire*, vol. I. Paris: Editions Gallimard, 1997.

Norris, Margot. "Narration Under a Blindfold: Reading Joyce's 'Clay.'" *PMLA* 102.2 (March 1987): 206–215.

Oates, Joyce Carol. "Lest We Forget." *The New York Review of Books* (July 19, 2007): www.nybooks.com/articles/2007/07/19/lest-we-forget/

O'Donovan, Louis. "John Carroll." *The Catholic Encyclopedia*. Vol. 3. New York: Robert Appleton Company, 1908. 28 Jul. 2016. http://www.newadvent.org/ cathen/03381b.htm

Percy, Walker. *The Moviegoer*. New York: Noonday, 1961, 1967.

———. *The Last Gentleman*. New York: Farrar, Straus, and Giroux, 1966.

Quallen, Matthew. "Georgetown, Financed by Slave Trading." *The Hoya* September 26, 2014. http://www.thehoya.com/georgetown-financed-by-slave-trading/

————. "Slavery Inextricably Tied to Georgetown's Growth." *The Hoya* October 23, 2015. http://ww.thehoya.com/quallen-slavery-inextricably-tied-to-georgetowns-growth/

Quinlan, Kieran. *Strange Kin: Ireland and the American South.* Baton Rouge: Louisiana State University Press, 2005.

Renan, Ernest. "What is a Nation?" Trans. Martin Thom. In Homi K. Bhabha, ed., *Nation and Narration.* 8–22.

Ricoeur, Paul. *Memory, History, Forgetting.* Trans. Kathleen Blamey and David Pellauer. Chicago: University of Chicago Press, 2004.

Rickard, John S. *Joyce's Book of Memory: The Mnemotechnic of Ulysses.* Durham, NC: Duke University Press, 1999.

Robbins, Bruce. *Feeling Global: Internationalism in Distress.* New York: New York University Press, 1999.

Rossington, Michael and Anne Whitehead, editors. *Theories of Memory: A Reader.* Baltimore: Johns Hopkins University Press, 2007.

Said, Edward. *Reflections on Exile: And Other Literary and Cultural Essays.* London: Granta, 2001.

Smith, Christopher J. "Blacks and Irish on the Riverine Frontiers: The Roots of American Popular Music." *Southern Cultures* 17.1 (Spring 2011: *The Irish*): 75–102.

Taylor, Lawrence J. "'There Are Two Things That People Don't Like to Hear about Themselves': The Anthropology of Ireland and the Irish View of Anthropology." In Waters 213–226.

Townshend, Charles. *Easter 1916: The Irish Rebellion.* London: Penguin, 2005.

Ulin, Julieann. "'Famished Ghosts': Famine Memory in James Joyce's *Ulysses*". *Joyce Studies Annual* 2011: 20–63.

Waters, John Paul, ed, *Ireland and Irish Cultural Studies.* Special issue of *South Atlantic Quarterly* 95.1 (1996).

Whitehead, Anne. *Memory.* New York: Routledge, 2009.

Winston, Greg. *Joyce and Militarism.* Gainesville, FL: University Press of Florida, 2012.

Yeates, Ray. "My Famine." In Hayden, *Irish Hunger* 191–200.

Yeats, William Butler. *The Collected Plays of W. B. Yeats.* New York: Macmillan, 1935.

Yerushalmi, Yosef Hayim. *Zakhor: Jewish History and Jewish Memory.* New York: Schocken Books, 1989.

Young, James E. From *The Texture of Memory: Holocaust Memorials and Meaning.* In Rossington and Whitehead 177–184.

Young, Robert. *Colonial Desire: Hybridity in Theory, Culture and Race.* London: Routledge, 1995.

1916: the Irish Rebellion. Documentary film by the University of Notre Dame's Keough-Naughton Institute for Irish Studies. 2016.

INDEX[1]

[1]Note: Page numbers followed by 'n' refer to notes.

© The Author(s) 2018   157
V. J. Cheng, *Amnesia and the Nation*, New Directions in Irish and Irish
American Literature, https://doi.org/10.1007/978-3-319-71818-7